LIFE-CONTROL

How to Assert
Leadership in Any Situation

CONTROL

SHELDON D. GLASS, M.D., M.Ed. with Harvey Ardman

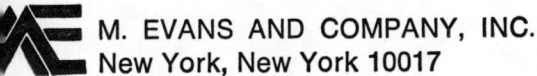
M. EVANS AND COMPANY, INC.
New York, New York 10017

M. Evans and Company titles are distributed in
the United States by the J. B. Lippincott Company,
East Washington Square, Philadelphia, Pa. 19105;
and in Canada by McClelland & Stewart Ltd.,
25 Hollinger Road, Toronto M4B 3G2, Ontario

LIBRARY OF CONGRESS CATALOGING IN PUBLICATION DATA

Glass, Sheldon D
   Life-control.

   1. Developmental psychology.   2. Small groups.
3. Social groups.   I. Ardman, Harvey, joint author.
II. Title.
BF713.G55   158'.1   75-44292
ISBN 0-87131-205-0

Copyright © 1976 by Sheldon Glass
All rights reserved under International and
Pan-American Copyright Conventions

Design by Joel Schick

Manufactured in the United States of America

9 8 7 6 5 4 3 2 1

CONTENTS

Taking Charge   3
Out of Control . . . Finding a Structure . . . Freud and Skinner . . . Content and Process . . . Who Is LIFE-CONTROL for? . . . The Benefits of LIFE-CONTROL . . . The Theory, in Brief . . . Complications and Complexities . . . Cycles Within Cycles . . . Group Speed Variations . . . People Variations . . . Phase Personalities . . . Leader Phase Personalities . . . Life Phases . . . Combinations . . . Learning LIFE-CONTROL

The Introductory Phase   29
A Case History . . . Introductory Phase LIFE-CONTROL . . . The Essence of the Introductory Phase . . . Four Miniature Phases . . . Unique Problems . . . General Problems

The Resistance-Testing Phase   79
A Case History . . . Resistance-Testing Phase LIFE-CONTROL . . . Finding Stability in the Midst of Change . . . Failing the Test . . . Four Miniature Phases in Resistance-Testing . . . The Transition . . . What Can Go Wrong in Resistance-Testing . . . Trying to Avoid Resistance-Testing . . . When Resistance-Testing Goes

Contents

on Too Long . . . Severe or Violent Acting-Up . . . When the Group Falls Apart or Gives Up . . . When to Call It Quits . . . Problems that Can Happen at Any Time

The Productive Phase 133
A Case History . . . Productive Phase LIFE-CONTROL . . . Judy's Life Phases . . . Productivity and Boredom . . Four Miniature Phases in the Productive Phase . . . Unique Problems . . . The Many Factors Behind Inefficiency . . . Task-Oriented Versus Relationship-Oriented Leaders . . . A Foreshortened Productive Phase: Restlessness . . . A Chance for Self-Improvement . . . General Problems

The Termination Phase 189
A Case History . . . The Essense of the Termination Phase . . . Four Miniature Phases in the Termination Phase . . . Unique Problems . . . The Termination Phase of Life . . . General Problems . . . Problems of Circumstance

Using Life-Control 229

To Lynn
FOR THE PRODUCTIVE PHASE

Acknowledgments

It is difficult to thank the people who contribute to the development of one's thought—for there are so many. But in particular I would like to thank my several mentors for sharing with me through the years their knowledge, enthusiasm, and the part of their life cycles that I had not yet experienced; the staff of the Glass Mental Health Center, for their loyal and steadfast support; my students at the Johns Hopkins University, for their repeated stimulation; the administrators and staff of those large (and small) government agencies, industries, and school systems that I have had the opportunity to work with; my patients, for unhesitantly teaching me what "process" was all about; Harvey Ardman, for his sincere dedication to the development of this manuscript; and above all my family, whose continual involvement has taught, supported, and enriched me beyond my fondest hope.

Sheldon D. Glass, M.Ed., M.D.

March 5, 1976

Taking Charge

Out of Control

Imagine what it would be like if you were able to predict, with complete accuracy, everything that would happen to you. Suppose you had every part of your life completely under control—that your every success was the result of your own careful and systematic planning, and that no mishap would ever catch you unaware.

Of course, that's not possible.

If you're like most people, you've been wanting to gain complete control of your life for as long as you can remember. You're doing your best to overcome the difficulties you may be facing in your family, your job, your friendships, and your other associations. You're probably spending a lot of time thinking about your problems and a lot of time confronting them directly.

But just when you feel you're getting a grip on things, something happens to upset you. Or just when you manage to get one area of your life in hand, another goes haywire. When things are at their worst, you feel tense, depressed, even helpless. Even when your life seems to be running smoothly, you may feel insecure about important decisions, past, present, and future. And the stronger these feelings are, the less you feel able to work out your problems.

Chances are the reason you haven't been able to take

charge of your life is that you don't fully understand what's happening to you. The triumphs of your life seem to be no more predictable than the disappointments. You're confronting a welter of information, experiences, and relationships, and you have no consistently effective way to make sense of them.

But it doesn't have to be that way. You can be in control of your life most of the time. You can gain that sense of stability and security so necessary to dealing with your problems successfully, and you can live your life without constant anxiety.

The answer lies in learning a system that will show you how to perceive the basic patterns in your life and how to apply the rules that govern them.

We can call this system LIFE-CONTROL.

Finding a Structure

Some time ago, I became convinced that there was an underlying process to life, a universal, identifiable pattern that repeated itself over and over again, that described and influenced most—if not all—human activity. The pattern appeared to be predetermined—that is, part of the natural development of every individual and group—and therefore usually predictable. With an understanding of the pattern, you could be better prepared to control your life and your activities.

Now, after years of work as a psychiatrist and educator, I think I have defined the basic elements of that structure. I've applied my theory to individual therapy, group therapy, workshops, seminars, and industrial and government consultation. I've used it to understand why individuals act the way they do. I've used it to analyze the workings of groups of all sizes, from marriages to nations. And it explains many things that don't seem to fit into other theories.

The process I've defined is an unconscious behavior pattern that humanity has developed during eons of evolution.

Its purpose is to help us cope with the changes and adjustments that are part of life, that we confront in our effort to have a satisfying, productive existence as we continue to develop.

When nothing interferes with this pattern, we move through life with relative ease, taking changes more or less in stride. When things go wrong, we may find ourselves stuck in one part of the pattern or another, out of control.

I set out to discover exactly what could go wrong with the pattern and why. I also looked for ways to prevent problems before they happened, if possible, or to solve problems that couldn't be prevented. What I developed was a system designed to help people understand what was going on in their lives and to help them regain control in those areas where they'd lost it. This system is LIFE-CONTROL.

Freud and Skinner

Many others have put forth theories of this sort before, of course. But most of them have built their theories on their understanding of either man's unconscious mind (Freud, Jung, Adler, and their modern interpreters) or the operant conditioning of behaviorism (Skinner and his followers).

LIFE-CONTROL explains how you function as an individual and within the groups to which you belong. It takes into account both your conscious and your unconscious mind. It helps to explain how people function separately and together. It is a synthesis and extension of what has been learned in the past.

The theory holds that man in his environment is a reflection of two different types of mental functioning—

1. The personal thought system: This is how you think about and deal with yourself as an individual, both consciously and unconsciously. I believe Freud has made the greatest contributions to our understanding of this system.

2. The social thought system: This is how you think

about and deal with your environment (and especially with other people), either consciously or unconsciously. I feel Skinner's model applies best here.

Content and Process

At its heart, LIFE-CONTROL is a way to see the patterns that govern your life and a way to influence them to your advantage. To learn the system, however, you're probably going to have to change your manner of looking at life somewhat.

For while most of us try as hard as we can to make some sense out of what's happening to us, while we take stock of the past and plan for the future we usually look only at the *content* of our lives.

By content, I mean face value. Content is the detail of life. It's what we work on, what we do in our spare time, what we argue about, what we read, what we feel, what we think. It's the substance as opposed to the dynamic.

We're occupied with content because that's what comes to us through all our senses. We're bombarded with it, via the media and the words and deeds of ourselves and others. It fills our consciousness, whether we want it to or not.

If you have a good understanding of the content of your life, you probably are quite self-aware. *But you can be self-aware without being in control.* You can have a good overview of the content of your life, but you'll be lost if you have no framework in which to put it.

That framework, the core of LIFE-CONTROL, is only accessible when you look at your life from another perspective: *process.* Process consists of patterns or structures, subtle trends and meanings that can be divined from content. It's what makes things work and happen.

The familiar cliché, "He couldn't see the forest for the trees," is a way of describing someone who's too involved with content to look at process. LIFE-CONTROL can show us a way to change our perspective.

Content comes in all shapes and sizes, from every direction imaginable, and in enormous quantities. No mind can grapple with it all without being confused. But if we're able to see life's processes, we won't be overwhelmed by its content.

LIFE-CONTROL is a way to perceive the processes that affect every aspect of your life. It's a way to put the content of your life into a manageable framework.

My research and experience convinces me that this framework is—

1. Inherent: It's not learned, not imposed by a leader or a set of written or unwritten rules; it is a predetermined, predictable process.

2. Universal: It describes and governs almost all activities, regardless of content or character, even when you're fully aware of it.

3. Necessary: It's a useful way to cope with the insecurity and instability that are ever present in our constantly changing environment.

Who Is LIFE-CONTROL For?

The precepts of LIFE-CONTROL are based on my analysis of how groups, their members, and their leaders function. If you think about it for a moment, you'll realize that there are few things you do—if any—where you're not acting as a member of some group or another. Whether or not you feel in control of your life will depend on what's happening to you in relation to the groups to which you belong.

When I say "group," I mean any conglomeration of *two people* or more. That deserves repeating, since I'm using this word in a special way. In this book, the word "group" refers to anything from a pair of lovers to an association of nations.

From everything I've been able to discover, the framework I've identified governs two-party groups (lovers, marriage partners, patients and therapists, buyers and sellers, etc.); families (both immediate and extended); classrooms (and schools and school systems); departments (or companies or even entire industries); social groups, either formal or informal; ethnic groups; even nations of all sizes.

The very same pattern describes the actions of groups of youngsters, adolescents, middle-agers, the elderly, or any combination. It underlies their actions, whether the group is composed of all males, all females, or any mixture. Further, the group in question can be spread out across the country (or even the world) or it can be all under the same roof. It doesn't matter.

What's more, the group can be only a temporary gathering (a company picnic, for example) or a permanent organization (such as the Red Cross). We all belong to many, many groups, even though we wouldn't always think of using the word "group" to describe our association.

There is one small class of groups to which LIFE-CONTROL may not apply, however. These are groups totally devoid of purpose, random collections of people, crowds, bunches These include people walking on the street, a train full of passengers, shoppers in a store, etc. Under normal conditions, they have no unified, cooperative purpose.

LIFE-CONTROL describes the processes that govern task-oriented groups, groups that have come together in hopes of achieving something specific. What? That depends on the group. A pair of lovers may have no greater purpose than giving each other pleasure. A family usually has as its purpose the protection and growth of its members. The purpose of a business group may be merely to do its job.

The task-oriented group's purpose may be as trivial as kite-flying or as momentous as the writing of a peace treaty. But if a group has a purpose of any sort, its activities can be described by the LIFE-CONTROL pattern.

We feel out of control when we can't handle events involving ourselves and our spouses or lovers, our families, our bosses or our jobs, our social groups, our classes, etc.

The precepts of LIFE-CONTROL, *however, can be applied*

by all group members and leaders, whatever the size and character of their group. So, unless you're totally out of communication with everyone, living in an igloo near the North Pole or on a desert island, LIFE-CONTROL can help you get a grip on things.

Two other terms you'll be seeing time and again in this book also need explanation, since they, like the word "group," are used in a special way. The first of these terms is "member" or "group member."

By this, I mean any participant in any group, or anyone whose actions affect a group, or anyone who is affected by it. Since you are a member of more groups than you can count, most likely, when I say member or group member, I'm talking about *you*. And I'm referring to practically everything you do.

The second of these terms is "leader" or "group leader." By this expression, I mean anyone who directs or guides a group's activities or anyone who exercises control over a group.

This term applies whether or not the leadership is shared, whether or not the group has willingly delegated the power of leadership, whether the leadership is fleeting or permanent, whether it is structured (one person is boss), or whether it is dynamic (shifting from member to member and from moment to moment). It applies whether or not the group even *knows* that someone is exercising control.

No matter how mild or meek you may think you are, no matter how isolated you may feel, it's my guess that you're the leader of one group or more. At the minimum, I'll bet you share leadership, or exercise occasional leadership, as you desire. So, when I use the word "leader," I'm talking about *you*.

But I'm also talking about you in a far more specific sense when I use that term, since you're now involved in learning the principles of LIFE-CONTROL. *Anyone who masters* LIFE-CONTROL *can assume a more effective leadership-role in his or her group.*

Let's take, for example, groups where the leadership is

fluid, where it passes freely from person to person, depending on who has the best ideas or who's more assertive. This describes many two-party groups, such as love relationships, marriages, friendships, worker-to-worker relationships, etc. It also fits those larger groups in which there is a rough equality among members, where there is no acknowledged leader.

A thorough understanding of LIFE-CONTROL will also help you to exert influence and even control over group with a structured leadership. These include businesses, families, formal social groups—or any body in which a leader is elected, appointed, or acknowledged by reason of personality or power.

LIFE-CONTROL will show you how to make a rigid leader share some of his authority with you, though he may not realize that's what he's doing. It will help you create a situation in which the leadership is less rigid and more fluid or dynamic.

Since most of your life and all of your interactions take place in groups, LIFE-CONTROL will enable you to foresee the most productive way to act. Knowing what to expect from each group, you'll know when—and how—to express your ideas, when to lie back and let others pursue their plans, how to handle disagreements, how to rekindle interest when it fades.

The Benefits of LIFE-CONTROL

This book is designed to teach you what LIFE-CONTROL is and how to use it. It will show you what the group process is, how to recognize it in every situation of your own life, and how to use your new knowledge to take charge of your life.

If you learn to think about your life in *process* terms, these are the benefits you can expect from LIFE-CONTROL:

- You'll learn to recognize what's actually happening in each group to which you belong and where you really stand in that group;

- You'll find out how to plan your future more intelligently and how to understand periods when every phase of your life is troublesome, or when you have no challenges at all;
- You'll discover a new technique to tell the difference between annoying, minor problems that will eventually solve themselves and major problems that will need your full and immediate attention—and how to prevent the former from turning into the latter;
- You'll learn how you can be a more effective leader at home, on the job, in your social groups, and among your friends—and how you can motivate people to work for you more enthusiastically;
- You'll find out what you can do, as a group member, to gain the greatest possible satisfaction from your participation and be of the greatest value to the group;
- You'll learn a new way of defining what kind of troubles are behind you, or nearly so, and which you should start getting ready for;
- You'll discover how to tell whether your job is really right for you and what to do about it if it isn't—short of quitting;
- You'll learn how to determine what kind of activities are most satisfying to your *process* needs and how to get involved in them; and
- You'll discover the patterns that govern your love relationships and learn how you can make those relationships go more smoothly.

LIFE-CONTROL, for all its benefits, is not a panacea. Its principles won't solve your money woes, your health problems, or any other content worries you may have.

But...

LIFE-CONTROL *will* show you how to isolate those problems from the pack. And it may very well give you extra energy and self-confidence by showing you how to view them in perspective, and how to deal with them yourself, as a leader.

The Theory, in Brief

By now, you're probably wondering what this new theory can possibly be. Actually, it's quite simple—at least at first glance.

I've found that every group (and its leaders and members) goes through an identifiable cycle, beginning with the moment it considers taking on a task or goal, and ending at the moment that task is completed or the goal is achieved.

This cycle is divided into four main phases:

1. The *Introductory Phase*

This is a period during which new goals are worked out and agreed upon. This is a time of excitement, even euphoria. Interesting, promising new things are about to happen. In a marriage, this is the honeymoon period. On the job, it's when the reorganization is announced. At the Elks' Club, it's when the dinner-dance committee is selected.

2. The *Resistance-Testing Phase*

This is when the group reacts with anxiety to the change that the new goals require, and it both resists that change and tests the leadership, to see if it can handle the process. This is a time of uncertainty, disagreement, and general travail. The status quo has been shattered and replaced by something less comfortable. In a marriage, this is that "period of adjustment" after the honeymoon is over, when conflicts and arguments appear. On the job, it's when people aren't adjusting well to the reorganization, when productivity has fallen off and absenteeism has risen. It's when the members of the dinner-dance committee start arguing over whether the main course, should be chicken or spaghetti, whether the dress should be formal or informal, whether there should be an orchestra or a rock band.

3. The *Productive Phase*

This is when the group works to accomplish the task and meaningful change takes place. It's when the arguments subside and goal-directed work begins in earnest. In a marriage, it's usually that moment when the conflicts that accompanied growing together are over, when the man and woman have worked out a mutually satisfactory division of labor, when they may decide to have children and settle down. On the job, it's when productivity begins to climb in the new department, when absenteeism is back to normal, when the group starts functioning as it should. It's when the dinner-dance committee gets on with the actual business of making plans and arrangements—hiring an orchestra, signing a contract with a caterer, renting a hall, etc.

4. The *Termination Phase*

This is when the goal is accomplished, the group consolidates its knowledge, and the cycle comes to an end. In a marriage, it could be when all the children go off to college, or when the breadwinner retires and the couple moves to a warm climate. On the job, it might be when that new product the department has been working on has finally hit the market. For the dinner-dance committee, it's when the event has been concluded, when the final postdance details are being cleaned up and the books are being closed.

Let me illustrate the theory another way, with a story. Suppose you have a two-week vacation coming and you want to go on a trip with your family. First thing you do is get them together and tell them what you have in mind. Then, you and your spouse, and possibly the kids, start talking about where to go.

You decide on a trip to Disneyworld, let's say. You plan to drive. The kids are wild about the idea, having never been there before. And it's going to be a nice change for their parents, too—no work, no cooking or housecleaning, and warm weather instead of snow. Everyone is looking forward to the trip. It's an exciting time.

What you're now going through, of course, is the *introductory phase*.

As the start of your vacation approaches, however, the family's mood changes somewhat. Your smallest child starts asking whether there'll be peanut butter at Disneyworld and whether he can take his teddy bear. The eldest worries about spending time away from her friends and her school. Your spouse wonders who will take care of the dog, whether the house will be secure from robbers, whether the car's tires are really safe, etc.

This negative mood is at its worst just before the trip starts. At that time, practically everyone in the family is grumpy and arguments—usually over nothing—erupt frequently. The smallest child starts crying when he finds out he can't take every toy in the nursery. Your eldest, who's discovered she's going to miss her best friend's pajama party, is very upset. Your wife keeps telling you that the weather is supposed to be bad in Florida in the coming week, and that she's sure Disneyworld crowds will be at their peak. And you're not too pleased with life yourself.

You're now going through *resistance-testing,* a necessary but not very pleasant part of the cycle.

Then, you all pile into the family car and drive off. For a little while, the bad mood continues. But before long you're driving through unfamiliar territory. Everyone starts looking out the windows at interesting things they've never seen before. After awhile, the littlest member of the family breaks out into song and everyone else joins in.

The weather in Florida turns out to be warmer, though not perfect. Disneyworld is crowded, but not so crowded you can't see what you want after a reasonable wait. The baby loses his teddy bear, somehow, but winds up liking a big stuffed Mickey Mouse even better. Everyone has a good time.

This is the *productive* part of the cycle. The goal, as originally decided, was to go to Disneyworld and have a good time. That's exactly what you're doing.

Finally, it's time to start home. You all pile back into the car and begin the trip north. No one's really overjoyed to see the vacation coming to an end, but the talk is about what was most fun, what didn't work out as expected, and how the family should spend the next year's vacation.

Now, you're in the *termination phase* of the cycle. The whole thing is coming to an end, but the group—the family—is consolidating and reinforcing what it learned and contemplating a new introductory phase.

Complications and Complexities

What you've just read is the simplest possible application of the theory, to the simplest possible example. Real life is much more complicated—and so is LIFE-CONTROL. To understand how to use LIFE-CONTROL in your own life, which is the purpose of this book, you'll have to put yourself on a "first-name" basis with its many complexities.

Most of these involve the deeper implications of each particular phase. I'll describe them and tell what they mean to you when I go through the phases in detail, in the chapters that follow.

But there are some complications that apply to all parts of the cycle. There's no better time to tell you about them than now.

Cycles Within Cycles

First, the four major phases I described in the vacation example aren't the smallest pieces into which the group process can be divided. Each phase is a miniature cycle in itself, complete with four miniature phases.

Let's take that again. Each phase—the introductory phase, the resistance-testing phase, the productive phase, and the termination phase—naturally goes through four smaller phases from beginning to end.

Thus, the productive phase, for example, has within it its own introductory phase, resistance-testing phase, productive phase, and termination phase.

The concept isn't as confusing as it may sound. Let's take a closer look at that vacation example and you'll see what I mean. As you'll remember, the introductory phase in that example began when the father told his family they were going on a vacation and it ended when everyone agreed on Disneyworld.

The introductory part of that phase occurred when the idea—taking a vacation—was introduced to the group. Everyone was excited and happy.

The resistance-testing part followed, however. Family members began to find objections to the idea: It would interrupt school, separate the family members from their friends, cause them to miss interesting events at home, etc.

The productive part of the phase began when the family stopped arguing and started talking about where they should go. Every member had his say.

The termination part of the introductory phase took place when the father said, "Okay, it's Disneyworld," and the rest of the family agreed.

Each of the other three phases could be analyzed the same way. And we'll do just that, in the chapters that follow. There, you'll learn—among other things—how to tell the resistance-testing part of the introductory phase from, say, the resistance-testing phase itself, and how to handle each.

Group Speed Variations

Groups don't spend the same amount of time in each phase. In my vacation example, I had the family touch bases at every phase, pausing more than long enough for us to see what was happening. It doesn't always work out that way in real life, however.

Depending on the composition of the group, how long it has been together, how different the present task is from the ones that went before, and what kind of leadership it has, some phases might be dismissed in a moment or two—almost before they could be noticed—while others might stretch out for, well, any length of time.

It's easy to imagine, for instance, how our vacationing family might have skipped the introductory phase almost completely. The father might have come home and said,

"Guess what? We're going to Disneyworld next month!" And the family might have reacted with a whoop of joy and some excited conversation, then started to pack.

In that case, the introductory phase would have been condensed (all four parts of it) into that whoop of joy and excited conversation. But it would have been there. The group couldn't function without it.

In the same way, the resistance-testing phase might have been truncated, if everyone were ready and waiting for a vacation. But some resistance-testing would have been inevitable. The vacation would have meant change, change would have produced anxiety, and the family would have expressed that anxiety (however gently) in resistance and testing, probably directed at the idea.

People Variations

So far, I've been describing a group in which all the members go through all the phases at the same speed. Everyone in my vacation example was in the introductory phase simultaneously, likewise the other phases. Usually, it doesn't happen quite that neatly.

In the average group, some members may still be in the introductory phase while others are in resistance-testing, for example. Or some may be in resistance-testing while others have moved on to the productive phase. It's even possible that some members may be several phases behind (or ahead of) others.

The effect of this is to make the phases overlap somewhat. It means that there's often no sharp division between, say, the resistance-testing phase and the productive phase (or any other pair). The group may flow from phase to phase, instead of taking distinct jumps. It goes through transitions.

In large groups, there may be enough out-of-phase members to join together and form one or more splinter groups. In smaller groups, there may be one or two members lagging behind the rest, or a couple of members far ahead.

There are many reasons individuals may lag—or sprint—through the phases in relation to their group. Often it's a matter of skill or experience.

If you haven't had a lot of experience with groups, or the particular task your group has tackled is totally unfamiliar to you (but not to the rest of the group), or if you're new to the group, you may not have the skills to keep up.

In my vacation example the youngest member of the family, the toddler, might not be able to contribute in the introductory phase because he doesn't really understand what a vacation is.

On the other hand, if what the group is doing is old hat to you (but not to all its members), you may race ahead of the inexperienced ones. The eldest child in my vacation-bound family, for instance, who's been on many a family vacation, might head for the guide books and maps at almost the moment the word "vacation" is mentioned, thus leaping into the productive phase while her baby brother is still trying to figure out why everyone is so excited.

But the reason for group members' uneven progress through the phases could very well lie elsewhere, such as in their personalities.

Phase Personalities

Some people can adapt with ease as their groups move through the phases. During the introductory phase, they become innovative. When resistance-testing comes, they criticize. When it's time for the productive phase, they get to work. And, in the termination phase, they reflect on the lessons taught by the cycle and get ready to move on to something new.

Most of us, however, are far more comfortable in one or two phases than we are in the others. We specialize, at least to a degree. We adapt only with some difficulty. So we go through the phases at uneven speeds.

This is a reflection of our psyches, as determined by

everything from the phase of our parents' marriage while
we were being brought up, to our heredity, to our life
experiences, even to the phase of our country during our
formative years.

If you were born when your parents were in the midst
of the resistance-testing phase of their marriage, you'll very
probably be a different kind of person from the one you
would be if you were born when your parents were in the
productive phase of their marriage.

Likewise, if you were brought up while your country was
in a resistance-testing phase—a time of riots and civil
disturbances, for example—you'll be different from those
who were brought up when your country was in a productive
phase—a time of no riots, no wars, no recessions; a time
when there was a positive atmosphere of cooperation and
coordination.

At any rate, some people turn out to be generalists
insofar as their ability to move from phase to phase is
concerned, and others turn out to be specialists. They're
really comfortable in only one phase. These people have
what might be called "phase personalities."

Put a person with a phase personality through any phase
but the one he's adopted as his own and he's edgy and
restless. Drop him into a situation in tune with his preferred
phase and he's snug and content.

We've all seen phase personalities of every variety.

Take, for example, the introductory-phase person. He's
the guy with a mind like a machine gun but very little
stick-to-it-iveness. He never has trouble coming up with
a new idea, but he's not the type to carry it through to
completion. He likes change for its own sake. He avoids
resistance. He dislikes drudgery.

The resistance-testing type is also a common figure.
He's the fellow who can always see the flaws in any
project. He can find mistakes, problems, or oversights
faster than anyone else. He might make a good troubleshooter for industry.

Or, he may be a troublemaker, an angry sort of person

who gets satisfaction from seeing things go wrong. Turn your back on him for a moment and he's doing something he shouldn't, or he isn't doing what he should.

The productive-phase personality usually isn't so colorful. He's the task-oriented man, the man who gets things done. He might not have many fresh ideas, but you tell him what needs doing and he'll do it. You don't have to worry about him shirking, or taking long lunch hours, or trying to pawn off the hard stuff on someone else. He's a bear for work.

The productive-phase individual also likes confronting and solving problems, particularly technical problems. He knows how to concentrate, how to bring his energies to bear on things that need fixing.

Then there's the termination-phase personality. He's the sort who enjoys reliving the past—and probably talking about it endlessly. He's not interested in rocking the boat or altering status quo. He's allergic to new ideas. He values stability and security above all else. He's a traditionalist.

In a group of any size, you're likely to see some pure phase personalities, some combinations, even some people for all phases. Just what positions they hold within the group may be vital to its smooth functioning. Obviously, if a termination phase-type finds himself in charge of thinking up new goals, the group is in trouble. Same with any other serious job/person mismatch.

Leader Phase Personalities

The speed and efficiency with which a group moves through its cycle will also depend on the phase personality of its leader, the most influential individual in the group.

The best leader, of course, is a man or woman for all phases, one who can provide the group with what it needs from the moment a task begins until it is completed. But other leaders have their place, too. And, if no generalist leader is available, the group can progress by changing leaders to match its changing phases.

The introductory phase-type leader is usually a man with ideas. And he knows how to get others thinking along new lines. He's not much for rules and regulations. He's only interested in the past for what it can contribute to the present and future. Such a man is frequently a charismatic figure. Politically, he's usually a liberal. In the extreme, he's a radical.

The resistance-testing leader is in many ways his opposite. He's concerned with control, with order. He sees his job as providing firm direction and guidance. He thinks about keeping his group's members in check, regulating their behavior if he deems it necessary, sticking to the letter of the law. This sort of man is usually a conservative. In the extreme, he's a reactionary.

The productive phase leader is a nuts-and-bolts man. He's an efficiency expert, a task-oriented fellow who knows how to get the job done. When he confronts a problem, his main impulse is to solve it, even if that means bypassing a larger, more important issue. He wants to get on with the work. This sort of man is most often a moderate. In the extreme, he's a technocrat.

The termination phase-type leader is a caretaker. His mission, as he sees it, is to preserve and protect. He's good at drawing lessons from the group's experience. By nature, he's a record keeper, accountant, or historian. This kind of person is generally a conservative, in the conservation sense. In the extreme, he's a curator.

Life Phases

Another reason a person might move unevenly through his group's phases is that these phases might conflict with his own "life phases." In the broadest sense, every person's lifetime can be looked upon as a cycle, complete with all the phases, in all their subtleties.

The introductory phase of life is that period between birth and the start of adolescence. It's a time of mental and physical preparation for the adult years of life.

The resistance-testing phase begins with adolescence, at around the age of eleven or twelve in the United States today. It's a time of restlessness and rebellion, when the struggle for independence from one's parents begins. For some people, this phase can last for decades.

The productive phase starts whenever adolescence finally ends. It's when the struggle for independence is over, at least internally, when the person begins construction progress toward his or her life goals. The start of this phase is often signaled by marriage, the birth of children, graduation from college, employment in a good job, or some combination. Most people spend the greater part of their lives in this phase.

The termination phase usually starts with retirement, or when age has taken its toll. It begins when the person has accomplished what he or she set out to do in life, or when the strength and energy necessary to pursue that goal are gone and the individual knows it.

Your life phase, just like your phase personality, if you have one, has a big effect on your value to the group and the satisfaction you get from the group. It may also be a factor in whether you linger in one phase (long after the group has moved on), or dart into a new phase (long before the group is ready).

Combinations

So far, I've been talking about what goes on in a single group. But we all belong to lots of groups—temporary and permanent, formal and informal, large and small, heterogeneous and homogeneous, close-knit and far-flung, voluntary and involuntary, one-time groups or on-going groups.

Without knowing you, I'd guess that you belong to at least the following groups—your family, your ethnic group, your graduating class in high school and college, your department at work, your career group, your religious group, your church, your clubs, your car pool or commuter group, your socioeconomic group, your political group, your sex group, your age group, your geographical group, your neighborhood group, your group of friends, your group of acquaintances, and—well, I think you get the idea.

Now, each and every one of these groups is going or has gone through the group process, the four phases. They're all at one phase or another. And you're participating in each group, in each phase, entirely apart from your life phase and phase personality.

Clearly, what's happening to you in one group can have quite an effect on how you feel in another, or perhaps all the others. This shifting, flowing combination of phases among the groups to which you belong will have a lot to do with how you feel about your life.

Let's say, for example, that you're in both the resistance-testing phase of your marriage and the resistance-testing phase of your job. Your life will probably be full of excitement, but unless you handle matters very skillfully, you may be in for some trouble.

Or, let's say you're in the productive phase of your marriage, the productive phase of your job, and the productive phase of your social relationships. You'll feel satisfied with what you're accomplishing and content, but you might find yourself becoming bored.

You may be in the productive phase of the most important areas of your life and the resistance-testing phase of some minor areas, or vice versa. But you're always finishing some activities and plunging ahead into others. You're always renewing your life by beginning new cycles.

It's not enough to figure out how one or two of your groups stand (unless they're the *only* groups that matter.) To get a grip on every part of your life, you should know what's happening in every major group in which you're a member.

And when you know that, there's one more factor you

can consider, the same picture for each of the people who has a major effect on your life—your parents, your spouse, your children, your boss, your best friends.

They, too, are participating in their groups. They, too, are in various life phases. They, too, have particular phase personalities. They, too, are affected by the combination of phases they must deal with in the combination of groups they belong to. They, too, are affected by others with similar problems.

To fully understand what's going on in your life, you must have a pretty good idea of what's happening in the lives of those people who are important to you. Before you have finished reading this book, you'll know how to do that.

Learning LIFE-CONTROL

To show you how LIFE-CONTROL works, in all its subtleties, I'm going to describe a number of case histories, composites drawn from my patients, friends, acquaintances, and my own life experiences. Names and identifying details will be changed, of course.

Using these case histories, I'm going to show you the process behind the content, according to my theory, phase by phase. I'm going to describe what went wrong, what went right, what might have happened but didn't, and why.

I'm also going to talk about the unique problems the people in each case history faced because they were in specific phases. And I'm going to talk about the general problems they faced that could have happened during any phase. Then I'm going to show how each can be solved.

In addition, I'm going to talk about the leader's role in each phase and the group member's role in each phase, and what effect other members and outside circumstances can have on each.

Let me emphasize at this point that when I use any of these terms—group, member, or leader—I'm talking about *you, your life, your groups,* and *your problems.* The case histories may not—probably won't, in fact—describe your situation exactly (though I've tried to find factors that are relatively universal), but the principles described will fit exactly, whatever your present position.

I know LIFE-CONTROL works. And I know you can make it work for you in any situation.

The Introductory Phase

A Case History

Philip and Marge Simon had lived in New York City for years. Their two children—Bobby, age ten, and Jenny, age thirteen—had both been born there. Both Phil and Marge had been raised in small towns, but they had always enjoyed the wide variety of stimuli New York constantly offered. Much as they enjoyed New York life, though, they had always dreamed of owning a home in the country. Philip and Marge had talked about country houses and managed to save some money for a down payment, but they'd never taken the first big step and begun to seriously look for a country place.

Then Marge found out she was pregnant. Even though it was midschool year for Jenny and Bobby, Philip knew that they'd have to begin thinking of moving since within not too many months their three-bedroom apartment would be too small for the four of them plus the new baby.

So one night after dinner Philip announced that it was time to begin looking for a house. The whole room lit up with excited conversation. Everyone had something good to say about the idea—life would be more pleasant, they could have room to stretch out, the air would be better, they would have a better life. They'd even have room, in an old country place, to bring Grandma Morgan, Marge's mother, in to live with them.

The family talked about the idea late into the evening. Philip even thought there might be some financial advantages, since Jenny and Bobby would no longer be attending private school.

The next morning, Philip quickly packed. He was going to Chicago for three days, on a business trip. In the apartment, there was an atmosphere of sweetness and light during breakfast. There was no question in Philip's mind that he'd hit on the right idea.

When he returned three days later, he wasn't so sure. Jenny and Bobby seemed sullen and angry. Marge didn't have much to say, either.

It turned out that they had been arguing in his absence. Bobby wanted the family to move to Gatesville, about fifteen miles southwest of the city, a suburb to which one of his former friends had moved.

Marge, on the other hand, wanted to move to Adamston, seventeen miles to the north. It had a beautiful new theater and a shopping center with branches of every major downtown store.

Jenny, ever the romantic, wanted the family to move out to the country, perhaps to a farm, at least to a pre-Revolutionary homestead.

Even Grandma Morgan had expressed an opinion, by phone. She wanted the family to move to Scranton, Pennsylvania, to be near the other relatives.

As for Philip, all he knew was that he wanted to get out of the city. He hadn't thought out where.

After dinner that night, the family discussed the subject at length, airing their feelings about each alternative. Philip put it all in perspective, by saying it was obvious they needed more information before they could proceed.

He pointed out they didn't know what houses cost, in either suburb or in Scranton or in the country. They didn't know what these places were really like. They didn't know about commuting times and costs.

Before the evening was over, Philip had worked out a

plan. They would take the next four weekends to visit the four spots the family had mentioned. And maybe they'd add a fifth trip if Philip came up with a place he wanted to investigate. That was the first part of the plan.

The only rule was that all possibilities should be considered—even Scranton, even chucking everything and moving to the country. Philip didn't think he was ready to give up his job yet. He certainly didn't have the money to retire and he wasn't very interested in job-hunting at this time in his life. But, for now, nothing was to be ruled out.

The second part of the plan was to get hard information about the four possible relocation sites. Bobby would get information about Gatesville (with Philip's guidance), Marge would find out about Adamston, Jenny (with her mother's assistance) would gather information on nearby rural areas. Philip would find out what he could about Scranton.

Meanwhile, Philip and Marge talked about his job. They kicked around the idea of leaving it, of finding something else, totally. But Philip was doing well and he was in line for bigger things. There were aspects of the job he couldn't stand—office politics, especially—but there were satisfactions, too, not the least of which was his substantial salary.

They worked through the fantasy of going back to the land and the dream of opening up a store or maybe a restaurant and becoming self-sufficient. Maybe the time would come when they could consider that, when the kids were older. But the time wasn't right yet, especially not with a new baby on the way. No farm, no Scranton. Philip and Marge communicated that decision to the children as soon as they made it.

Now they were down to three suburbs; Philip added in his own choice, Crystal City, only forty-five minutes by train to midtown. The family spent the next Saturday exploring that little town, however, and no one liked it —not even Philip.

That left Adamston and Gatesville. The family, under Philip's direction, did as complete a research job as they could on the two towns, comparing taxes, schools, parks, shopping, commuting time, town services, zoning regulations, and neighborhoods. The crime rates were low in both places, the air clear and sweet, the schools modern and progressive, the streets clear, the children seemingly happy and carefree, the commuter trains modern and well maintained.

The Simons talked extensively to real estate agents in both suburbs and spent many a weekend out of the city house-hunting. It was a preview of coming attractions everyone enjoyed.

In the middle of May, a real estate agent in Gatesville showed them a big old white clapboard house with two acres of lawn and trees, at the dead end of a winding, sidewalk-free country lane. It was love at first sight.

The house cost a bit more than Philip and Marge had planned to spend, but they couldn't turn it down. To the entire family's relief, and with everyone's agreement, he signed a binder.

Everything was settled.

Introductory Phase LIFE-CONTROL

What you've just read is a simplified, condensed version of the Simon family's decision to move out of the city, the introductory phase. As it happened, they went through this period reasonably smoothly. Without knowing it, they followed the precepts of LIFE-CONTROL.

It might not have happened that way. There were many opportunities for trouble and conflict. Wrongly handled, the whole project might have collapsed at several different points.

In the pages that follow, I will discuss what pitfalls the Simons sidestepped, what shoals they avoided, and how.

It's important to remember that this case history illustrates only the beginning of the cycle. After making the decision to move, the Simon family had to go through three more phases before it accomplished its goal:

It had to face a resistance-testing phase during which every member of the family expressed his or her anxieties about the coming change, a productive phase during which the move was actually made, and a termination phase during which final details were cleaned up and the family settled in its new home.

I chose this case history because I felt that you'd understand what the Simon family was going through from your own experience. But I might just as well have described the introductory phase of:

- A young married couple's first serious discussions about having a child;
- A meeting of the Ajax Bag Company's management on bringing out a new line of plastic bags;
- A NATO foreign minister's conference on war plan revisions;
- A man and woman talking about getting married; or
- A college English department talking about new teaching assignments.

My point is that I could have used any introductory phase *content* from any group with any goal to show how the *process* works. To get the most out of the following analysis, you should substitute your group—your family, your department at work, your social group, etc.—for the Simons. The principles will be identical.

But back to the Simon family.

The Essence of the Introductory Phase

What actually happened during the introductory phase of the Simons' decision to move out of the city?

It all started, you'll recall, with Marge's pregnancy. That rekindled Philip's desire to move out of the city. When Philip introduced that idea to his family, everyone reacted with interest and excitement.

With the idea of leaving the city in front of them, the Simons were at first almost euphoric. They felt a sense of power, as if they'd suddenly found a way to solve all their problems. Then they took a closer look at the idea and discovered that they each had different ideas about it.

If these disagreements had been serious enough—if no one had been willing to compromise between the suburbs and the country, for example—the process might have stopped right there and not resumed until someone suggested a place everyone liked.

No one in the family happened to be that stubborn. Faced with differing opinions, they soon started exploring their options, refining the basic idea, conceptualizing once-vague needs and goals.

During this time, each member of the family got to know how the others felt about the idea. They also learned how their leader, Philip Simon, operated in this new circumstance (though they probably had a good idea how he'd do things from previous experience).

With everyone still eager to move out of the city, Philip weighed the facts as he saw them (including the feelings and opinions of the other family members) and made up his mind: He decided on the big white house in Gatesville.

Then he got the others to agree to his decision, which was easy because it was their decision, too. And the phase ended when the family committed itself to making the move, when Philip signed a binder and put down a deposit.

Emotionally, the introductory phase is marked by interest, excitement, even euphoria—depending on the group's make-up and the character of the idea under discussion. It's a honeymoon period, with little serious conflict, in which everyone is anticipating pleasure, satisfaction, or rewards to come.

This certainly was the case with the Simon family, who came to see a house in the suburbs as the ideal solution to its problems.

Substantively, the introductory phase is marked by no

real change. Nothing actually happens. The lives, habits, and psychological sets of the group members are disturbed by nothing more than a new idea. Its realization is in the future.

At the end of the introductory phase, the Simon family was still living in the city. They'd committed themselves to a course of action, but hadn't actually taken the first step.

Four Miniature Phases

The introductory phase, like all the rest, is divided into four parts. Here's how they looked when the Simon family decided to leave the city:

1. *The introductory part:* This began when Philip seriously introduced the idea of leaving the city. They showed interest, enthusiasm and excitement.

During this period, group members may have doubts, fears, and disagreements concerning the new idea. But they usually hold their tongues, because everyone else seems so excited. Any oppostion to the new idea is usually gently expressed, often disguised in "devil's advocate" language.

2. *The resistance-testing part:* In the Simon family, this started soon after Philip left on his business trip. Each member of the family had his or her own idea of where they should move to and they all started arguing about it.

At this point in the introductory phase, the group hits a little snag. As it starts to seriously consider the idea, doubts appear, problems surface, disagreements come out. Reality intrudes into the dream.

This is the first major test of the project. And the testing is directed against the idea itself (rather than the leader). The leader himself can participate in testing the idea. In later phases, he'll be its chief defender.

If there's too much opposition to the idea, the cycle may end here. There'll be a return to status quo until someone introduces a new idea and a new cycle starts. If the majority of the group—or its most important members—accept the basic idea, the group will start working toward its new goal.

The Simon's disagreements were not serious. They were able to consider alternative suggestions. In doing so, they moved on to the next segment in the cycle.

3. *The productive part:* For the Simons, this began when the family started doing serious research on its alternatives, when family members started getting information about their favored relocation spot, when exploratory outings were planned.

During this time, the group sets out to solve the problems it uncovered during resistance-testing. It refines the original concept and alters it as necessary. It selects good parts of the idea and eliminates bad parts. It spells out its basic goals in considerable detail.

At this point, the group will study the project's feasibility in depth, in terms of its resources, abilities, and the time-frame that applies. When it finishes, the group should have a plan for accomplishing its goal. It is a very enthusiastic time.

4. *The termination part:* The introductory phase came to an end for the Simon family when Philip put a deposit down on the Gatesville house, with the group's approval. That deposit amounted to a solid commitment on the part of the family.

Commitment is the essence of this segment of the introductory phase. The goals have been thought through and refined. Each member has had his say. No fatal flaw has been found in the idea.

Now the group decides to go ahead and do it—to undertake meaningful change.

What I've outlined above is how the process works when the introductory phase goes well, with no major problems. But life is full of problems. And the process I've been describing can be blocked, prolonged, foreshortened, halted or distorted by almost any one of them.

On the other hand, the process also contains within it the solution for most of the difficulties that can disrupt it.

Unique Problems

Each phase in the cycle is subject to particular, unique problems. In the introductory phase, the main ones are the inability to conceptualize, not enough discussion, and too much discussion. Each problem has its consequences, causes, and cures. All are quite closely related.

The Inability to Conceptualize

Many a group gets into a situation that calls for new ideas, but no new ideas are forthcoming. Or, the germ of an idea surfaces, but can't be developed into a realistic possibility.

If a group attempts to go forward on that basis, it will wind up with no clear goals, no well-defined objectives, and not very much chance of accomplishing its aims.

If the Simons had been afflicted with this problem, they might not have been able to come up with anything other than stopgap solutions to their problem—a bigger apartment, bunkbeds, roomsharing, etc.

Or they may have come up with the idea of leaving the city and finding a house, but been unable to develop it, unable to think out where they'd like to live instead, unable to figure out how much they wanted to spend, and so on.

Problems in conceptualizing can crop up for several reasons:

1. *The group doesn't have enough information.* Let's say that the Simons have been city dwellers all their lives. They don't know anyone who lives in the suburbs or the country and they can't imagine what living there would be like. In that case, they'd be unlikely to come up with the idea of leaving the city. Or, if they did, they wouldn't know what to do next.

This is the hardest conceptualization problem to identify, because a group has to *know* it doesn't know. But it's the easiest problem to solve, once identified. It's just a matter of getting the needed information.

If this is your problem, you'll very likely feel insecure with the idea you and your group are pursuing. You may be confused about how to proceed. You won't feel as though you are on solid ground.

The solution is to get more information. Find out how others have handled similar problems. Come up with alternative ideas. Examine your resources to see what strengths can be brought to bear.

Let's say you want to learn how to type. You can march yourself down to your local college and sign up for the first opening, without a further thought. But if you did that, you wouldn't be thinking your idea through. That would require finding out where typing is taught, at what hours, over what period, when classes begin, and for what price. You couldn't really follow through until you had that information.

You'll know when you can stop hunting for information. You'll feel like you know what you're doing and where you're going. You'll have a sense of security and self-confidence. You and your group will start coming up with all sorts of modifications, expansions, and additions to the original idea.

2. *The group doesn't have the necessary skills.* Let's say that the Simons simply aren't accustomed to making decisions on a family basis. In fact, they really haven't had many big decisions to make.

If so, the younger members of the family in particular might not have the necessary intellectual and perhaps emotional skills. They might not know how to take part in a meeting, how to assert their opinions, even how to gauge their feelings.

This can happen anywhere, in any group. A reporter added to the staff of a newspaper, for instance, may not have the intellectual skills he needs to comply with the city editor's request for a "five-hundred-word weather short with a fresh angle." Or, he may not have the emotional skills to see his copy edited and rewritten by someone else. Or, he may not have physical skills to type it up by deadline time.

In the classroom—and I've seen this quite often—youngsters from disadvantaged backgrounds may simply not know how to conduct thesmelves. They may swear, throw things, fight, ignore the teacher, or otherwise misbehave—not because they're bad, but because they don't have the skills necessary to perform in a classroom situation.

Any group members who lack the skills needed to participate in the group's activities are likely to be not simply a neutral influence, but a negative one. And nothing can kill new ideas faster than negative vibes.

If you're the leader of such a group, or you want to exercise your powers of leadership, there are three LIFE-CONTROL remedies you can use:

First, work with those members of the group who have lower skill levels. Include them whenever possible. Show them that you value the abilities they do have. Guide them and teach them greater skills—individually at first, if need be. Reinforce their assets; above all, show them respect.

Second, practice. Set up a modest situation where little is at stake, then put the group's unskilled members (or the whole group, if every member is unskilled) to work on it. Help those people who don't know exactly what to do by providing a model for them, or give them direct guidance.

Third, create a structure. Add elements that will move the group along the desired path, such as formally going around the room to elicit everyone's opinion or view, or holding votes on various questions, or making lists of plans or problems. Let the group know what they are going to do and why, and how that fits into the larger picture.

Your guidance and instruction will help improve the skills of the inexperienced group members, probably to the required level. Practice will help them internalize those skills and perfect them. And structure will give them a sense of security.

These changes should help transform unskilled group members into skilled group members, thus enhancing their ability to make positive contributions to the group's goal, which in the introductory phase involves coming up with and helping to develop appropriate new ideas.

3. *The group (or its leadership) is conditioned to traditional thinking.* Let's say that the Simons dearly love their city apartment because it's rent controlled, or it's a co-op or a condominium and they bought it after extensive research only three years ago and have enjoyed living there, or either Philip or Marge has lived in the building or nearby since childhood.

In those circumstances, the Simons wouldn't be very likely to come up with the idea of leaving the city. This thought would be beyond their basic frame of reference.

Traditional thinking influences all kinds of groups, large and small. In the 1920s, for example, the U.S. Navy's top brass watched Billy Mitchell and his bombers destroy a number of old warships, yet still refused to believe that air power was a threat to their principal ships. In all fairness to the top brass, though, the traditionalist of an organization helps to give the organization stability, and no change from tradition should be made without considerable care.

Some people simply don't have the freedom within themselves or within their organizations to do things or think about things in a different way. They have either consciously or unconsciously elected to limit their choices, in order to maintain their feelings of—what else?—safety and security.

So long as they stay within their chosen boundaries or frames of reference, all is well. Once they step outside, or are exposed to new ideas, they begin feeling threatened or insecure.

To some extent, this is a function of age. Younger people, less locked into established frames of reference than their older counterparts, are often more flexible and adaptable. They are more receptive to change. Their elders, more organized and settled, are often hostile to change.

In fact, this difference leads to a natural antagonism between the two groups. The elders often feel younger people are unsettled, wild, ready and willing to consider anything. The younger people often think their elders can't change, even when change is called for.

But all of us feel threatened by change to one degree or another. For this reason, groups follow a specific pattern to keep feelings of insecurity to a minimum.

I call this pattern "the natural path." It's an important element of LIFE-CONTROL. I've seen groups follow it hundreds of times, both in person and when analyzing tapes of group activities.

Following the natural path, groups will initially discuss peripheral issues, subjects that are at best tangentially connected with the main question. After awhile, they'll move on and start talking about the question itself, but from a third-person perspective: "They did this," "It happened to them," etc.

As they become more comfortable with the new idea, they'll begin discussing it in the second person: "You should do this," "Don't you think that. . . ." Finally, when they feel quite secure, they start sharing feelings and experiences on a first-person basis.

In our case history, the Simons took to the idea of moving out of the city like a duck to water. They got into a first-person discussion quickly. But if the family had felt less secure, they might have started talking about the city's growing suburbs, or its new shopping centers, or life on a farm, or the rising crime rate.

Then, they might have discussed what happened to some neighbors or friends who'd moved out. Once comfortable on that level, each family member might have talked about how the move would affect the others. ("You won't have to worry about walking home from school any more,

Bobby," or "It's so safe in the country they leave their doors unlocked.")

Finally, when they were sufficiently comfortable, they'd talk about themselves, about their feelings, needs, opinions, etc. ("I won't mind the commute if the train is on time," or "It'll be fun riding my bike down a country lane.")

I've described the natural path at this point because it contains a LIFE-CONTROL concept that can be used to slowly ease a tradition-bound group into personally considering a new idea, without violating its need for security.

When a group feels secure, the members can express their personal feelings about the subject directly, openly, and spontaneously. For example, most families provide a feeling of security; most family members are willing to "tell it like it is." The difference between a business meeting and an encounter group is that in a business meeting you should allow the group to develop in its natural path. Often the group members will talk about peripheral issues first, and begin to express personal feelings as time and the security of the group permit. In an encounter group, the leader confronts the members about their personal feelings from the very beginning, circumventing the natural path and increasing the anxiety of the group members.

Of course, some groups are secure enough to express their personal feelings from the very start, some groups are never secure enough to, and some groups never should try.

Let me illustrate with an example:

Virgil Eckhardt, head of shipping at a large retail mail-order house I'm familiar with, retired and left the firm. Management took the opportunity to replace him with a bright young man named Frank Sigfrid, former assistant head of shipping at a nearby electronics outfit.

The company chose Sigfrid because he knew everything there was to know about modern shipping methods—computerized routing, automated packing, containerization, etc. Management felt the department's staff was very competent, but had no one with Sigfrid's know-how or management skill.

A week after Sigfrid started his new job, he held a staff meeting. "We're going to modernize everything," he told his men. "We're going to start from scratch and make ourselves the best shipping department in the business." He outlined all of his modernization plans, in a sort of pep talk.

If Sigfrid is to maximize his modernization program, he will have to recognize two things. First, that he does not have a meaningful relationship with his men at this point. Specifically, they cannot relate their personal feelings about the change until a feeling of security and trust is established. Second, he will still have to go through the resistance-testing phase even after the group feels secure enough to express their feelings.

Utilizing the natural path can help Sigfrid develop a meaningful relationship with the group members. First, he should sound out his group, get its feelings on modernization. If he does, he will quickly see he is surrounded by stubborn, old-hat thinking. That established, he should carefully and consciously guide the group along the natural path, even stretching matters out, if necessary.

Sigfrid can make sure the group spends plenty of time talking about peripheral issues, any subjects that would make them feel comfortable with him, before moving on to a direct discussion of modernization.

Then he should talk at length about what other companies had done, describing both pros and cons, inviting others to contribute what they know. After that, he can discuss his own experiences, what happened when the shipping department at the electronics firm was modernized.

Finally, when he is fairly sure that everyone is comfortable discussing the concepts, he can bring the discussion slowly around to first-person issues, talk about what each staff member will be doing in the new setup. If he meets opposition, he can back off and stay with second- or third-person issues until the group is ready to go on.

This technique, by itself, might not be enough to give the shipping department staff the sense of security they need to start considering modernization. In that case, Sigfrid can apply another LIFE-CONTROL technique.

He can introduce the modernization in many small steps, rather than one giant leap. He can make each step only a slight modification of previous practice, and not go on to a new step until the last one is thoroughly absorbed and accepted.

If most of the Simon family or one of its leaders (Philip or Marge) were tradition bound, the leader (or member) who wanted to get the family thinking about leaving the city might start by talking about stopgap solutions to their problem—a larger apartment, more doubling up, etc.

The object here would be to introduce the idea of change on a level the tradition-bound family would find acceptable. Once they were comfortable with this sort of change, the leader might go on to suggest moving to a better neighborhood, then to the area's outskirts, etc., never moving too fast for the family.

4. *The group (or its leadership) is afraid to risk conflict.* Let's say that the Simon family conducts its own private war every night, using words for weapons. Or, let's say that Philip's relationship with Marge is rocky.

In that situation, it's not hard to imagine Philip keeping his mouth shut about his new idea, for fear of setting off an even more violent battle or endangering his already fragile relationship with his wife.

If he does bring up the subject, these fears might cause him to be so purposely vague about it that no one can possibly object, since it isn't definite enough. Or, he might bring it up in such an offhand way that no one is really aware that something new is being seriously suggested.

This sort of behavior is apparent on the work scene, in the classroom, even in social groups. It's easy to imagine an employee proposing an idea very carefully, in the hope of getting his boss's approval; likewise, a new manager, meeting with a group of experienced employees, or the new president of the YMCA about to suggest an addition to the building to a membership already griping about new, higher dues.

People often hold back on ideas this way, in hopes of making them objection proof, either in the formulation or in the manner they're presented. The problem is, that's impossible. And it prevents any new idea from taking hold and getting developed.

Every time change is suggested, every time status quo is threatened, all members of the group will feel some anxiety. Sooner or later, they will express this anxiety, by resistance-testing.

Resistance-testing is a normal, natural, unavoidable step in every phase. If properly handled, it can be made to flow smoothly; if bungled, it can be made more difficult. But it can't be eliminated.

And yet, people have an understandable urge to sidestep friction, if possible, sometimes even to the extent of remaining silent when they should be saying something.

The cure for this type of conceptualization problem involves the essence of LIFE-CONTROL. It's a matter of becoming aware of the process, of accepting the notion that some degree of resistance-testing is inevitable whenever any new idea is introduced, no matter how it's presented, no matter how it's structured.

If you recognize that resistance-testing is an integral part of every phase, you should lose some of that reluctance to bring up and discuss a new idea. You should also be in a better position to handle the resistance-testing that will follow (but more on that later).

Not Enough Discussion

Sometimes, a group that is quite able to generate and conceptualize new ideas and new goals never gets the chance, because its leader or one of its members steps in and imposes an idea by fiat.

The group that goes ahead on this basis is in trouble, though it may not seem so at first. Since the members were not given enough time to make their views known, or to explore or test the idea, there is no way they can wholeheartedly commit themselves to it.

It's like a football coach telling his fullback to take the ball through the left tackle slot and "mow 'em down," even though the fullback has been dumped behind the line of scrimmage five times straight with that very play.

He'll go out there, all right. He'll take the hand-off from the quarterback. He'll move out behind his blockers. But his heart probably won't be in it.

If Philip Simon were a different sort of man, his family might have found itself in that situation. He might have said, "I thought it was time we got out of here, so I put a deposit on a house in Gatesville. It's exactly what we need."

If someone objected, saying, "Wait a minute. Don't we get a chance to say where we'd like to live?" he could have replied, "I've given the whole matter a lot of thought and this is the best place, believe me."

By strength of personality, status, or position in the group, a person can force acceptance of the idea he favors, sharply curtailing discussion, squelching open opposition. He can do this gently or harshly, for personal reasons (he's the only one who really understands the problem, say), or for the "good of the group" (the decision has to be made in a hurry for some reason, for example).

He may succeed in putting his idea into effect simply because he's worked it out more completely or more clearly or more quickly than anyone else. Or, there may be no rival ideas on the floor.

It seems that we have a strong man here, exercising his strength, or a dominant personality acting as he's accustomed to acting. But this kind of behavior actually indicates weakness in most cases. The group member or leader who imposes his ideas on the rest of the group without permitting discussion is usually trying to avoid conflict or testing. He believes that his idea, or his status, might not survive a challenge.

But there is no way to eliminate resistance-testing. If you try to drive it underground, like the dominant individual I've been describing, it will continue to bubble up, disrupting the group again and again as the group staggers toward its designated goal.

Group members who never get a chance to test the goal or task laid out for them, who must commit themselves to a new idea without having an opportunity to express their feelings about it, will harbor a smoldering discomfort, frustration, or anger.

The LIFE-CONTROL solution? If you're the leader of your group, let it have its head during the resistance-testing part of the introductory phase. Or, if you're not, encourage your group leader to do so. The path to control, in this case, is *not* to control, at least not overtly.

You may be saying at this point, "Wait a minute. Do you mean I should *never* impose an idea on my group? Shouldn't I do something if they just keep talking and talking and talking and never decide on a course of action?"

You certainly should. And that brings me to the introductory phase's last unique problem.

Too much discussion

We've all participated in groups that never decide on anything. All they do is consider the alternatives. Commitment never comes.

The group that acts this way may wind up with a definitive list of the pros and cons of any number of ideas. Its members might fully air their feelings, several times perhaps. But it won't accomplish its goal. It probably won't even define it clearly.

Many a decent idea has died this way in Congress. A legislative proposal might be submitted to the House, then assigned to a subcommittee for further exploration. After interminable hearings, it might move on to a committee.

There it might be the subject of more interminable hearings. Then it might simply vanish and be reabsorbed, possibly to appear the next year and perhaps suffer the same fate.

The Simons might have talked endlessly about getting a house in the country, finding good points and bad points in the idea. Then they might have talked at length about living in the suburbs, without reaching any conclusions. Then they might have debated the pros and cons of moving to another city, etc. Or, they might have discussed all of these ideas simultaneously, without reaching a decision.

This can happen for several reasons.

It may be, for example, that there is *genuine disagreement* within the group and that no one faction is stronger than another. Philip might want to live in the suburbs, Marge in the country, and neither might be willing to compromise. Or, one may love the city too much to leave it.

Or, it may be that the group is simply *too afraid of change* to commit itself. The Simons may be too locked into their way of life in the city—to its conveniences, to its cultural advantages, to its excitement, to their city friends—to risk moving out, even if that's the obvious solution to their problems.

Or, it may be that the idea simply *isn't practical*. Perhaps the Simons just don't have the money necessary to buy a house in the suburbs. Or, maybe the commute would be just too inconvenient, making it impossible for Philip to spend enough time with his family every day.

In that case, no amount of talk will lead to action. The conversation is just wishful thinking, or planning for the fairly distant future.

It may be that the *leadership can't handle the changes* required by the next project and the group knows it. Maybe Philip is having a bad time at work and doesn't have the time or energy to deal with the tensions of a big project like moving. Maybe he and Marge have been having their own troubles lately and the relationship couldn't bear the strain of any major change. Maybe one member of the family or another is mentally or physically ill.

Or, maybe the family is already faced with *too much change*. Maybe Jenny is going into the resistance-testing of adolescence with a vengeance. Maybe Philip is about to change jobs. Maybe the problems with Grandma Morgan are too upsetting or too costly.

Any one of these factors, or any combination, could cause the Simons to discuss the new house idea forever, never coming to a decision.

When a group talks and talks about a new project and nothing happens, the first thing it should do, from a LIFE-CONTROL standpoint, is ask itself some content questions:

1. Do we really want to do this?
2. Is it practical, or at least possible?
3. Do we have the necessary resources (time, energy, funds, manpower, etc.)?
4. Are we relatively free to concentrate on the project?
5. Are our disagreements resolvable?

If most of the group answers "no" to one or more of these questions, chances are the project will never get off the ground. And maybe that's best, at least for now.

But let's say the majority of the group answers "yes" to all the questions. In that case, the reason for the group's inability to commit probably lies within the process, not with the content.

To go back to our case history, imagine that the Simon family really wanted to leave the city, that it had the resources required, that nothing made the move impossible, that no other major projects diverted its energies, and that the family members, whatever their differences on the subject, were willing to compromise.

Then imagine that the Simons still could not reach a decision, that all they could do was sit around and mull over the possibilities, talking endlessly. We've all been in groups where this has happened. What's the explanation?

There are really several possibilities. The most likely are:

- The family is going through the resistance-testing part of the introductory phase, but expressing itself in a passive-aggressive manner, stalling and delaying rather than testing.

This might be because of a lack of confidence in or anger toward Philip Simon, the family leader. And these feelings may have nothing to do with the present project.

- The family is trying to avoid resistance-testing, by attempting to anticipate all problems in advance, thereby eliminating any possible source of conflict.
- The family or several of its members don't have the necessary intellectual or emotional skills to reach a decision.

These explanations should sound familiar, since they're also responsible for some of the other problems unique to the introductory phase. All three of them can be handled by the LIFE-CONTROL techniques I've already described. It's mainly a matter of providing the necessary security.

If you're the leader of a group that is talk-talk-talking instead of moving toward a commitment, and the reason has to do with process, not content, you can:

1. *Create a structure within which the group can operate.* Set up a timetable, hold a series of votes, or formally parcel out work assignments. Make lists, draw up charts, do whatever you can to put matters in order, so the group can feel a sense of control.

This is exactly what Philip Simon did when he came home from his business trip to find his family upset and confused over the idea of leaving the city. He assigned work to various family members, set up a plan of attack to help explore alternatives, and found other ways to structure the task at hand.

2. *Get more information on the issue.* Do research, get expert advice, talk to people who've already done what you're trying to do.

You can distribute this information to the entire group (if it can absorb and use it). This will increase the group's sense of security.

Or, you can use the information to make yourself more expert. This will also increase the group's sense of security, since it will see you as being more capable if you can answer its questions.

Or, you can do both.

Philip Simon also used this method. He immediately set out to get more information about where the family might go, after leaving the city. He had each member of the family working on the project. But he retained the ultimate control and exercised his leadership.

3. *Get the group to practice making decisions on lesser issues.* If the main question is simply too overwhelming to be considered, or beyond the skills of most members of the group, you can start them off on smaller decisions.

Philip Simon might have done this, had it been necessary, by getting the children, for example, to help him set up a schedule for visiting likely suburbs. Or, he might have done this by having his wife draw up a list of things she'd like in the new house.

If you succeed in giving the group a sense of security, it will usually move through the introductory phase in a normal, orderly manner, coming up with new ideas, testing them, working them out in detail, then reaching a decision.

Incidentally, that decision won't necessarily be to go ahead. The process can just as easily lead to a red light as a green light. That depends on content.

General Problems

The Simon family, like any other group in the introductory phase, must deal not only with the problems unique to the phase, but also those that could happen at any time —general problems.

It could have difficulties in the leadership area (Philip might not be a good leader), or among its members (Jenny or Bobby, or even Marge might be implacably set against moving), or circumstantial problems (Grandma Morgan might, in the midst of everything, get sick and require costly medical care, making a move financially impossible).

In this section on general problems, I intend to deal with all three of these categories, as they affect the introductory phase. I'll also take this opportunity to discuss general problems that have general cures; that is, problems that can be treated more or less the same way, regardless of phase.

Please bear in mind that when I refer to the Simon family, or when I use the terms group, member, or leader, what I'm saying can be applied directly to your life situation. In a very real way, I'm talking about you.

Whether or not you think of yourself as a member of a group, you are—and of many groups. Whether or not you see yourself as a leader, you probably have been at one time or another, either exercising sole leadership, or sharing it, or occasionally acting as a leader. Or, you are such a leader right now. Once you've mastered LIFE-CONTROL, you will be a more effective leader.

Leadership

That said, let's start with the leader, the most influential member of any group, and in our case history, Philip Simon, the head of the family.

Every group needs a leader. That includes a group of children playing, a detachment of ditchdiggers, a religious group, a group of boat-disaster survivors on a life raft, a family—you name it.

The leader may have a title—president, chairman, boss—and may be chosen by some formal means, or he may be tacitly acknowledged by the group without any discussion of the subject, like Philip Simon is the acknowledged leader of his family or the co-leader along with his wife, Marge.

Groups can start without a leader, to be sure. But then their first order of business is usually to select one. This has been proven by countless experiments by clinical psychologists.

Exactly why groups need a leader is too complex to

discuss here. But there's no doubt that they do. It's inherent to the group process. In fact, leadership is so essential to a group that it is very unlikely to destroy its leader, at least in normal circumstances.

Let me repeat that, since it has so many LIFE-CONTROL implications: Groups rarely destroy their leaders, even when those leaders aren't doing such a good job. Leaders are pulled down only when they jeopardize the group, its members, or its very reason for existence.

The movie (and book), *The Caine Mutiny*, is a good example of this principle at work. The senior officers of the U.S.S. *Caine* put up with a great deal of bad leadership from their commander, Captain Queeg. He was arbitrary, weak, inefficient. When they finally replaced him, however, it was because he'd jeopardized the ship and its mission and showed every sign of doing it again, totally without warning.

Though a group is hesitant to destroy its leader, it isn't so hesitant about attacking him. It will frequently attack, sometimes fiercely. But, eventually, the majority of the group will come to support the leader, unless he badly mishandles the situation. Groups inherently respect the position of leadership, if not the person who's filling it. And they will bend over backward to preserve their leadership.

All kinds of books and articles have been written about what sort of personality makes someone well suited to leadership. But from the work I've done with literally hundreds of group leaders, I've learned that personality isn't the key to leadership.

I've seen extrovert leaders and introvert leaders, charismatic leaders and conservative leaders, soft-spoken leaders and blunt leaders—all of whom were equally effective in their respective groups.

What makes a person able to lead effectively, then?

He must have three particular qualities, I believe:

1. *He has to be comfortable with himself.* In the Simon family, leader Philip Simon has a certain inner steadiness

and calm. And this is reflected in his style of leadership. He's very much at ease with himself. His actions are natural and comfortable.

His family reacts to this style by adapting to it. When he came home from that business trip and found his family upset and confused, he almost automatically started putting events in order. And his family fell into line without a struggle. They adjusted their behavior to his style.

Philip Simon could have been another sort of man altogether, though. He might have been quiet and withdrawn, very uncomfortable with conflict, for instance. Given that personality, if he'd forced himself to mediate between the members of his family as they argued about where they wanted to live, he would have been very uncomfortable. And he probably wouldn't have been very effective.

If, on the other hand, he'd let the family discuss the move openly, allowing them to adapt to his style of leadership rather than trying to change himself to meet their needs, things probably would have worked out well. A leader simply can't change to please everyone, unless the group is totally homogeneous.

2. *He has to convince the group he's capable of handling whatever comes along.* If the leader cannot project a sense of capability, the group may not feel secure enough to work toward its goals.

Let's take Philip Simon again. If his family had grave doubts that he could handle the changes and challenges intrinsic to moving, they'd be very unlikely to commit themselves to the project. If they did, they'd be saying they could go it alone, without a leader. And groups don't do that.

If, on the other hand, the Simon family believed that Philip could cope with and adapt to whatever changes and challenges he might face during the moving process, they'd probably cooperate and go through the cycle smoothly. He'd be an effective leader.

It all boils down to this: The more a leader can project a sense of capability, the more of a leader he is. And the reverse is also true: The less of a sense of capability a leader projects, the less of a leader he is.

3. *He must be sincerely interested in his job and in the members of his group.* The group leader who displays these qualities is likely to get strong support from his group even when he runs into trouble or makes a mistake.

Philip Simon demonstrated his concern for both the task at hand and for the other members of his family by actively soliciting their opinions, and by assigning them to tasks that fit their talents and interests. As a result, when commitment time came, they backed him 100 percent.

If you're the leader of your group, there's no substitute for showing your sincere interest in your group and your concern for your job from the very first. But the best opportunity for displaying these qualities may come when you make a mistake. (And you will—every leader does.)

Groups rarely expect their leaders to be infallible. But they do expect them to be honest. So, when you make a mistake, the first thing you should do is admit it. The leader who admits his mistakes, and then takes sensible corrective action, simultaneously proves that he's committed to doing his job well and that he takes seriously the interests of the group members.

We've had two spectacular examples of this on the international scene in recent years. One came after the Bay of Pigs disaster, the unsuccessful invasion of Cuba. President Kennedy admitted his mistake on nationwide TV, took responsibility, and was rewarded by a surge in the popularity polls. Another happened after the 1967 Arab-Israeli war. Egypt's President Nasser admitted his mistakes and resigned. He was swept back into office by popular acclaim.

(Of course, Nasser was the only leader in view and the Egyptians—like any group—needed a leader, especially after their military defeat.)

Besides proving his sincerity and honesty, the leader who admits a mistake also demonstrates his capability anew. True, he may have been guilty of bad judgment. But he had the good judgment to see he'd been wrong.

The leader who doesn't admit his mistakes rarely fools anyone in his group and his dishonesty breeds a lack of confidence in him, not to mention bitterness and anger. As a result, the group is less likely to succeed.

Even though "honesty is the best policy" works, it won't nullify a string of serious errors. Eventually—though later than you'd expect—the group will start shopping around for a new leader, if the errors threaten the group, its members, or its goals.

Of course, I can't tell you how to deal with all the content issues of your life. But I think LIFE-CONTROL can help you avoid most of the process errors you're likely to confront if you're a leader or about to become a leader.

This information will also be extremely valuable to you if you're a group member. Knowing what a leader can do wrong or what flaws he can have that can complicate a group's orderly progress through its cycle, and how those problems can be corrected, will help you better understand your position in the group and what you should do.

Leader Errors and Flaws

1. *Absence:* Groups not only need leaders, they need them to be around and visible. This is particularly true in the introductory phase, when a group is just getting started, and in difficult times, such as the resistance-testing phase.

If no leader is present at these crucial moments, the group members become more anxious. Their testing and acting-up increase. They ask for guidance in many different ways. And the effect is the same if the leader is there but unwilling to fulfill his role, if he withdraws or refuses to participate.

This is exactly what happened to the Simon family during the touchy resistance-testing part of the introductory phase of their moving project. Philip Simon got them going, by presenting the exciting (and threatening) idea of leaving the city. Then he promptly took off for a business trip.

While he was gone, the family's differences blossomed.

They began to think of alternatives and problems. Conflict erupted. But once he was back on the scene, the family settled down and quickly entered the productive part of the phase.

In the racial riots of the late 1960s, New York City escaped relatively unscathed. One major reason for this was that Mayor John Lindsay, the city's leader, made it a point to walk the streets with various well-known community figures. He showed everyone that the city's leadership was on the scene and active. And it worked, since there's no better way for a leader to provide stability in times of crisis than to be immediately and directly available.

But what if you must be absent for a time? It is possible for a leader to delegate some authority. Simon might have told him family, "If you have any questions about the idea, Marge will listen to them and answer them if she can. I'll be back on Friday and we can discuss everything in detail then."

Eventually, though, the leader must be personally available, since the final responsibility lies with him. That's what makes him a leader.

2. *Inexperience:* Inexperienced leaders come in two main varieties—the ones who don't know much about the group's content problems, and the ones who haven't had much practice at leading groups.

Of the two, the least likely to fail or to cause problems of his own is the leader unfamiliar with the group's content. He can always learn. That's what so many business executives do when they switch industries. It's a matter of using familiar skills on new subject matter.

But the person who finds himself in a leadership role even though he's had little previous leadership experience is in a much more difficult situation.

I have a case history that will show you what I mean:

About a year ago, on a hot August night, Harold Baum, the dynamic producer of the eleven o'clock news on a local independent TV station, suffered a serious heart attack. He was rushed to a hospital and put in the intensive care ward.

After three days there, his doctors said he had an excellent chance for a full recovery, but that he'd have to stay away from his job for at least six weeks.

The station management then asked Baum's twenty-six-year-old assistant, John Gaudio, to take over responsibility for producing the news show. Gaudio had never produced a TV show on his own before, though he'd been assistant producer of another news show in Iowa before he came east.

Though Gaudio was very inexperienced, the station management actually had very little choice about putting him in charge. There was no one else on the staff who could do the job. Gaudio knew the staff and the routine. Certainly, he was no Harold Baum, but management felt he should be able to keep things going during Baum's absence. And just in case he didn't work out, the station's vice president began to look for a more experienced man.

In situations like this, many a young man has not done well, unable to handle either the work or his subordinates. Some have learned what to do, and even how to do it, but they haven't been able to convince the rest of the group of their leadership abilities. Their youth and inexperience has been too great a factor.

In some respects, John Gaudio was lucky. Both in Iowa and in his current job, he'd seen topnotch leaders at work. He'd watched qualified and respected men and seen how they operated.

He'd also been lucky enough to see ineffective leadership. While he was in college, he had worked for the school's radio station. Its manager didn't care about the student volunteers who made the station work and he made his feelings clear at every opportunity.

Gaudio had also seen other leaders at work—his father, the principal in his high school, the factory foreman for whom he'd worked one summer, the president of his fraternity, and several others. Putting his experiences and observations together, he had a pretty good idea of what effective leadership was. The night after he was appointed temporary producer of the news show, he thought about the leaders he had known and considered their strengths and weaknesses.

If you find yourself in Gaudio's situation, the chances are you'll have the same resources he did. At the very least, you've been a member of several other groups. You've seen many leaders at work. Whether or not you're aware of it, you've picked up some useful ways of thinking about leadership. To apply them to your current situation, you should start by consciously examining what you already know about the subject.

Despite his knowledge, Gaudio felt anything but secure in his new position. And he knew he couldn't go very far in communicating his insecurities to his subordinates, or they'd lose all confidence in him. The best antidote to his insecurity, he correctly realized, was more information about both content and process.

As it happened, Gaudio knew several other assistant producers in the city or nearby, men he'd met at school, people who had been with his station and moved on, or those he had known socially. He contacted everyone he thought might help and asked if he could watch them on the job, then get their advice on his own situation. Almost everyone agreed.

If you find yourself in a situation similar to Gaudio's, you can do the same thing. You can get more information about your group's content problems by studying other, similar groups or by doing research on the problems you know you'll be facing. This will give you increased expertise in the subject, which will enable you to handle your group's problems more effectively while winning the respect of the group members.

You can also get more information about your group's process problems by finding out how similar groups and their leaders have handled similar difficulties. This knowledge should substantially boost your self-confidence, since you'll be better able to anticipate problems and have at least partial answers already in mind. It will also bolster the group's confidence in your leadership capabilities.

But I have found that the best source of information is the membership of the group. When working with families, government agencies, and school faculties, I rarely asked a question that one or all members of the group could not answer, or at least provide significant information to help answer the question. Inexperienced leaders like Gaudio hesitate to expose their lack of knowledge. But as they become more confident as leaders, they don't hesitate to say to their colleagues, "I don't know the answer. What are your ideas?" or "How about some help?"

Despite his increased knowledge and self-confidence, Gaudio knew he couldn't succeed without the wholehearted cooperation of his subordinates—the cameramen, lighting men, sound men, editors, writers, set designers, and the others who brought the show to life. So he set out to share his responsibilities with them as much as possible.

Gaudio met privately with his main subordinates, telling each one he knew he had a difficult job on his hands and that he needed all the help he could get. He assigned one man who had an unusual talent for getting the most from his co-workers to be his assistant. He assigned another, who was exceptionally alert to production foul-ups, to be his troubleshooter, giving him the responsibility for finding flaws in the show's presentation and coming up with solutions. He gave the anchor man, a calm, clear-headed type, responsibility for seeing that the other on-camera performers kept to a tight schedule.

In each case, Gaudio fit the increased responsibility to the man's skills and temperament. His object was to get his subordinates behind him, to gain their support. But he was also hoping to utilize his subordinates' special skills, to keep the program's quality high, even to improve it if possible. He wanted them to be as involved as possible.

Sharing responsibility when possible is an excellent idea for any leader. That way, he can enlist the support of older, perhaps more experienced group members, while getting their expert help and advice. Another way to share responsibility is to make the group more democratic. The leader can do this by getting the explicit approval of a majority before taking any major action.

But a caution is in order here. If you're a new or inexperienced leader, you should remember that you can only go so far in sharing your leadership. Sooner or later, if you keep doling out responsibility, the group won't know if you're a leader or just a member. When that happens, you're in for serious trouble. You can share some of the responsibilities of leadership. But to be effective, you must retain the trappings, the status, and the final decision-making power, and everyone in the group should know it. You must also maintain a certain social distance from the rest of the group. You can be "one of the boys" on special occasions and you can operate as informally as you want, so long as everyone is aware of your position.

3. *Overdominance:* A leader's lack of confidence often shows itself in a tendency to be dictatorial, to beat down opposition and impose his will when decision-time comes, even if the decisions are trivial.

This tactic is based on the false assumption that resistance will vanish when it can't be expressed. Resistance, as I've said, is inevitable. If it can't be openly expressed, it will show up in disguise.

This happened to an acquaintance of mine I'll call Sam Hertz, vice president and sales manager of a medium-sized manufacturer of women's ready-to-wear clothing. When the recession hit, the company's business fell alarmingly. Sam and his partner agreed that if the current trend continued for another six months, they'd be bankrupt and out of business.

So Sam called his entire sixteen-man sales force in from the field for a meeting. He laid it on the line without flinching: Either everyone met his quota or he started looking for a new job. Sam said he was sorry, but that's the way it had to be. Then he ended the meeting abruptly, having said everything he'd planned to say.

Before a month was out, two of Sam's best men had quit and gone to work for a competitor. A third was in the hospital with a bleeding ulcer. A fourth got himself arrested for drunk driving, then vanished. Only three of the sixteen had met their quotas for the month.

At that point, Al Gold, one of the three who'd succeeded, dropped in on Sam. "Maybe we should look at the territory assignments again," he suggested, "or maybe we should discuss the discount schedule, or even re-examine the line."

Sam would have none of it. The old system had worked perfectly in the past and it would work perfectly now. It just required a little more effort. Gold tried to press his point, but laid off when Sam began to get angry.

It took eight months, but Sam's firm finally went broke, and just as the recession began to lift. It needn't have happened that way. Sam's company fell victim to his bad leadership as much as it did to bad economic conditions.

What Sam didn't do was let his sales force react to his ultimatum. He didn't let them speak out, argue, object, or do anything that would allow them to discharge their anxiety and become more comfortable with the new situation. By acting the way he did, he encouraged his salesmen's doubts about his leadership.

Whenever a leader says, "This is what we're going to do," in such a way that the idea can't be criticized, or even explained, group members are going to find some way of expressing their anxieties, of resistance-testing. They may quit, they may make serious errors, they may keep pestering the leader for more instruction, they may go off on a tangent. But they won't just docilely fall into line, without a whisper of trouble.

Unfortunately, Sam didn't know the principles of LIFE-CONTROL. In a way, it's hard to blame him for what he did. He was in a panic. And he didn't want the group to know how helpless he felt. So he exercised what he thought was tight control over the meeting. Actually, that "tight control" was a symptom of his insecurity and his sales force probably recognized that, at least subconsciously.

If Sam had let them discharge their anxiety over the new

situation, by speaking out, or objecting, or reacting, or making suggestions, or criticizing the operation, and so on, chances are the sales force would have been able to come to grips with the new circumstances under which it was operating.

The salesmen probably would have raised process or content issues that Sam could have dealt with. He would then have had a chance to demonstrate his leadership abilities. And the meeting might have come up with some positive suggestions about achieving the goal, keeping sales up.

If you're a member of a group whose leader is acting this way, about the only thing you can do is to try to show him the error of his ways. If he can see that his actions are counterproductive and alter his approach, it may save the whole group a lot of grief.

But if you have suggestions to make, don't wait until the troubles begin. The time to present ideas is in the introductory part of any phase. If you wait until the resistance-testing part comes before you speak up, your suggestions may be perceived as just that much more troublemaking.

That's what happened when Al Gold tried to convince Sam to re-examine some other areas of the firm's operation. Instead of listening, Sam saw Al's suggestions as just another sign of difficulty or acting up.

4. *Overreaction:* Leaders who don't understand the group process, either consciously or unconsciously, may unwittingly push the group into stronger-than-normal resistance-testing and keep it there. This happens when a leader reacts to resistance-testing the wrong way—*by taking it personally, by getting angry and defensive.*

I've often seen this happen in the classroom. Students invariably test their teachers. They talk, pass notes, ask to go to the bathroom every ten minutes, laugh when the teacher's back is turned, etc.

When their teachers either don't understand the process, or they don't have the inner security to allow the class to test yet retain their equanimity, they frequently overreact.

They come down on the testers with both feet. The result is continued testing, stronger than before and sometimes amounting to an entire year of disruption.

But if the same teachers discipline the class appropriately, then make it clear that there are limits beyond which the class may not go and stick to those limits, the testing usually vanishes after awhile and the class gets down to business.

This problem is less common in the introductory phase than it is at some other times in the cycle, mainly because group members usually don't test the leader then. They normally test the idea. Still, an insecure leader can overreact at this time.

Philip Simon, for instance, might have overreacted when he came back from his business trip only to find his family at odds over the house-hunting project. He might have punished the kids for arguing and berated his wife for not keeping things under control in his absence.

If he'd behaved that way, his family probably wouldn't have been very cooperative when he finally said, "Okay, now let's start thinking about that new house again. Only this time, no bickering."

I'll explore this subject in more depth when I get to the resistance-testing phase. But, for now, remember this: When the members of your group start resistance-testing, the best thing to do may be nothing at all until you know exactly what you're doing.

5. *Expectancy:* Very often, a leader can sabotage his group merely by his attitude. If he's sure they won't be able to accomplish the task, for example, and he doesn't bother to hide his opinion, he's sharply reducing their chances of success.

The reverse can also happen. Leaders can often inspire their groups to remarkable accomplishment if they believe the group can do the job and they make their belief evident to all. Many a football coach has turned a collection of losers and misfits into a powerhouse by expecting great things of them.

It's all a matter of—here we are again—security. The group whose leader believes in them makes them feel less anxious in the face of change, more capable of handling events. The group whose leader has grave doubts makes them feel more anxious, less able. Good expectancy, then, will lead to an increase in productivity; poor expectancy, to a decrease.

Let's go back to the Simons to see this in action. Imagine that Philip Simon had assigned members of the family to look into moving alternatives, as he actually did, but with reluctance and evident skepticism. Chances are they'd do a slipshod job.

Expectancy, then, is an important element in control. The leader who understands the group process can use it to turn on the members of his group and get more out of them than might normally be expected.

6. *Out-of-phase leaders:* If, in its introductory phase, the group finds itself with a leader who can inspire new ideas, who's willing to let group members test, and who is capable of making a commitment, it can hardly ask for better.

(Such a man or woman might turn out to be the best leader of all, one who can move easily through all the phases, but unless the group has had prior experience with its leader, only time will tell whether a leader is genuinely flexible.)

The group might very well find itself not with the ideal leader for its phase, but with someone who's out-of-phase, either by reason of personality or life circumstance.

Their leader could turn out to be a resistance-testing-type, a man not inclined to let members of his group brainstorm and go off in all directions—which is what's needed in the introductory phase—but, rather, someone concerned with order and control.

If Philip Simon were such a man, he might have put the idea on the table after he'd thought it out in detail, then kept a watchful eye out for dissenters and the faint-of-heart, ready to bring them into line.

Or, the leader might be a productive phase-type, a man

who has little patience for talking about a project, even to explore alternatives and variations, who wants to get on with the work. He, too, wouldn't be willing to spend much time exploring new ideas.

If Philip Simon were that sort, he might have driven the family out to a suburban real estate office and started everyone looking at houses immediately. If they reacted by making other suggestions about other suburbs or the country, he would have been annoyed because time was being wasted.

Or, the leader might be a termination phase-type, someone who's more interested in the past than the present. He'll want to preserve the group and keep it functioning, not subject it to the risks involved in taking on a new project. If that description fit Phillip Simon, he wouldn't have been the one to come up with the idea of leaving the city.

If someone else had suggested leaving the city, Philip (if he were a termination phase-type) would probably have come out against it, either overtly or covertly, strongly enough to scuttle the idea, but not so strongly as to excite conflict or introduce instability into the group.

If you're a member in a group in its introductory phase and your leader is out of phase, what can you do? What LIFE-CONTROL techniques apply?

Let's assume, for a moment, that the leader is essentially permanent, like Philip Simon (or anyone formally appointed, or in the midst of his given term). In that case, you and the other members of the group have several options:

1. You can try to ease the out-of-phase leader into a well-defined introductory phase, either by providing structure, or by taking the smallest possible steps forward. This might work with a termination phase-type leader, someone who doesn't want to rock the boat. It might provide the security he needs.

2. You can attempt to convince the leader to step aside, to delegate leadership to someone else. (Philip Simon might, say, put Marge in charge of house-hunting if encouraged to do so by the rest of the family.)

If a resistance-testing-type leader could be made to feel

he had clear lines of authority over the temporary leader and could pass judgment on the project after the group thought it through, he might accept this concept. But he'd have to have a solid sense of control.

3. The group might split into subgroups, with one of the subgroups working through the introductory phase of the cycle, developing ideas, testing them, and finally presenting one or two to the entire group, or to the leadership. Of course, a full-scale introductory phase would then begin, but that's the whole idea.

This might work in the case of a productive phase-type leader who doesn't want to "waste time on outlandish schemes." He might allow a few members of the group to devote their energies to the idea, if only to "get it out of their systems" while he busies himself with the group's main continuing activities.

Jenny and Bobby, for instance, might be the ones who want to leave the city, not their mother or father. However, if they pester enough, Philip might say, "Go ahead, find out all the facts. Then tell us what you've found out."

Which of these alternatives is possible, if any, depends on specific content circumstances and on the personality of the leader. They also require joint action by at least part of the group.

Group members in this situation have one more alternative (assuming they find the present setup unbearable): They can quit the group and set up one of their own.

Temporary leaders, or those whose status depends on the good will of their group, usually informal leaders in informal situations, present the same list of alternatives, plus one: The group can always rebel if the leader is sufficiently out of tune with group desires and replace him, either gently or not so gently.

However, once a leader's position is acknowledged and accepted by the group, replacement is relatively uncommon, unless, as I've said, the leader jeopardizes the group or its reasons for existence, or its members. Even then, replacement is a slow process in most cases.

If you're a leader and you know you're out of phase with the group, you have three choices, essentially: Be flexible and adjust to the flow of the process; step back and allow someone else to take over temporarily, until your preferred phase and the group's coincide once more; or relinquish leadership permanently.

Member Problems

In a sense, most of the member problems I'm about to discuss are also leader problems; that is, the leader must solve them if the group is to go through its cycle smoothly and efficiently.

1. *Low skill level:* Some groups are composed of people who've been through the process many times, perhaps together, maybe even under the same leadership. Such a group will probably be able to handle a new task with aplomb.

But many another group is either partly or entirely composed of members who have rarely worked together in groups, who simply don't know how to perform their roles. This is usually more of a problem in the introductory phase than later, since by the time the group has moved on members who started out with low group skills have learned a great deal.

In groups with low skill levels, the leader must be more directive than in groups that already know what they're doing and how to do it. He must provide constant guidance. If necessary, he should instruct the members on what's expected of them.

This is especially true if the group is mixed, if some of the members are highly skilled and others aren't. In such groups, the members with low skill levels will probably have a negative self-concept. Unless they can be brought up to snuff, they'll never make meaningful positive contributions to the group and they could very well cause a lot of trouble.

In our case history, Bobby, the ten-year-old boy, could easily have been missing the necessary skills to fully participate in the project. In that case, his father should have recognized this and helped, by giving him work he could handle, by telling him what was expected of him, by showing him what to do, by taking the boy under his wing.

2. *Isolation:* Some people, even while members of a group, become (or remain) isolated. Sometimes these people cause trouble for the group, sometimes they don't.

Let's start with the isolated group member about whom the leader needn't worry. This is the person who is normally withdrawn. The group knows this is his normal behavior—he's not trying to make some point—and so does the leader. Everyone, including the person who's isolated, is comfortable with his behavior.

Usually, it's not hard to identify such a person. He's quiet, but he doesn't stand out. He doesn't try to draw attention to himself. Actually, an apparently isolated person in the introductory phase may turn out to be a highly productive group member later on. He may be absorbing everything that's being said.

In the Simon family, for instance, Jenny, the thirteen-year-old girl, may have sat through the introductory phase without uttering a word, as she usually sits through every discussion. But she might have understood everything that was brought up. When the time comes to move, she might be a hard and willing worker.

Very often, though, the person who's isolated within the group is very uncomfortable. He may feel insecure and be afraid to participate. He may have a poor self-image and actually fill certain psychological needs by having others angry at him. He may be misplaced in his group, his knowledge and skills much lower, or higher, than that of his colleagues.

Some people isolate themselves not by nonparticipation, but by trying to dominate the group, by talking too much, by trying to do too much. The group gets angry at this individual and isolates him psychologically.

Group leaders cannot ignore such isloated members. They can cause too much trouble. For one thing, the isolated member might divide the group, causing some to defend him, others to attack him, and all to forget the goal. For another, he might upset the leadership, if he sees his actions as a challenge.

Something like this could easily have happened to the Simon family when it began to consider leaving the city. Jenny, for instance, might have withdrawn from the discussion altogether, angry that her country living idea was vetoed so quickly.

The family might have reacted by catering to her, trying to draw her out, doing everything to please her, only to find that their efforts drove her deeper into her shell.

She might have felt, with reason, that if she withdrew far enough, the group would reverse itself, consider her ideas, maybe even adopt them. And this tactic might have angered Philip Simon, if he saw it as a challenge to his leadership and an effort to sabotage the family's goals.

What can a leader do in a case like this? He should take this behavior as a request for guidance and direction. He should let the isloated member know what's expected of him. Also, he should make every effort to see that the nonparticipating member feels a part of the group. He should recognize the member for his own ability, for what he can contribute.

It's not always possible to bring an isolated member back into full participation, however. Some members do not have the ability to perform at the level of the group and can't or won't be taught. In that case, the leader must proceed as best he can, taking care not to let the isolated member retard the group or damage its chances for success.

3. *"Elopement"*: Another problem member, particularly in the introductory phase, is the person who drops out very quickly, who leaves the group before it really gets going.

Two types of people act this way: the misfit, who really doesn't belong in the group by reason of different interests or different skill levels; or the potential leader, who can't tolerate being a follower.

The best thing a leader can do for the first type of person

is to try to integrate him into the group. If that's impossible, the leader should refer him to a program better able to meet his needs. (But if he's an integral part of the group, like a runaway child, he should be brought back in if possible, supported, involved in group projects, and if necessary, taught the skills he needs.)

The second person is too valuable to lose. He's the man who has been defeated in an election, who has lost out in a leadership struggle, who has been passed over at promotion time not because he lacked merit, but because someone else had more. He can be a very productive person, if properly supported.

The way to deal with such people is to give them as much responsibility as possible, to let them know you respect their abilities, to delegate authority to them, putting them in charge of subtasks and so on.

This, in part, is what John F. Kennedy was doing when he selected Lyndon B. Johnson to be his running mate in 1960, after their bitter struggle over the Presidential nomination. In fact, it's one of the reasons for the office of vice president, or right-hand man, in many organizations.

In the case of the Simon family, the problem member might turn out to be Philip's wife, Marge. In most ways, they probably share leadership of the family, with Marge taking charge in some areas, Philip in others. If they're to get along, however, and to help each other to the maximum, each must recognize the other's position and abilities, whoever's temporarily in charge.

4. *Out-of-phase members:* Every group from two people on up will have members who are at least partially out of phase with the group's phase and that of the other members. Until people are identical, that's inevitable. The good leader will identify these people and be sensitive to their needs and their effect on others.

In the introductory phase, some members, by reason of personality or life phase, might not be exactly suited to the task at hand, because they're inclined toward resistance-testing, production, or termination.

The resistance-testing personality, for instance, might make it very hard for a group in the introductory phase to make a commitment. His constant criticism of every new proposal may keep the group talking and talking until it's obvious no conclusion can be reached.

If you're the leader of a group that has such a member, you can usually count on the group to tell him when they've had enough. If Bobby Simon were that sort of person, his mother and his sister would eventually tell him they weren't interested in hearing any more complaints from him.

In some groups, however, where conventions or rules don't allow the members to criticize one another, you may have to be the one who sets limits. In that case, let the member speak his piece, but make sure others get their turn, too. If he keeps on attacking after he's had his say, he may need special attention.

Depending on the content you're working with, there may be a way to give him some additional responsibility. You might assign him to identify the problems the group will face if it follows a certain course of action, and ask him to come up with possible solutions. Or, you might put him on another task altogether.

The challenge here is to see the group member not for his liabilities but for his assets. Before you consider dropping him or bypassing him, or strictly disciplining him, try to find a way to use his talents.

If you must criticize, do it in private. That way, the member won't have to show the group he can stand up to you. He'll be far more able to accept what you say. Further, the rest of the group won't start worrying about the possible public humiliation to which they'll be subject, if they err.

In the end, however, extreme solutions might be needed, such as setting limits in front of the group, bypassing, even dropping the troublesome member from the group. As a leader, your criteria for these actions should be the same as the group's criteria for ousting its leader: that the actions of the person threaten the group, its members, or its reason for existence.

The Introductory Phase

The productive phase-type of person in a group's introductory phase presents a very different sort of person. He's not interested in talk. He doesn't want to generate and develop new ideas, but to get on with the work. When the group finally gets into the productive stage, he'll be one of its most valuable members.

The productive phase personality isn't likely to disrupt the group when it's in the introductory phase of a cycle. But if he's frustrated enough with the lack of real action, he may drop out.

To avoid this damaging loss, you must handle such a person with care and sensitivity, with extreme awareness of his needs. He wants to be working, so, if you can, give him work to do—specific, worthwhile tasks that will occupy him and make him feel he's being useful.

The Simon family was lucky to have members flexible enough to participate fully in the introductory part of its first phase, then move through resistance-testing into the productive part of the phase.

It might not have happened that way. Marge, for instance, might have been far more inclined toward production. She might have longed to decorate a house, to pick out fabrics, carpets, and wallpaper. That might have dominated her thoughts while everyone else tried to figure out whether the family should move to the country or the suburbs, then to which suburb.

To keep her interested and involved, Philip might have suggested that she start getting an idea of furniture prices, find out the name of an interior decorator and meet with him, and explore the other ideas that interested her.

True, all of this would be premature during the introductory phase. It could even turn out to be wasted energy, if the group were unable to make a commitment. But, if the group did follow through the cycle, Marge's work would eventually be invaluable.

The termination phase-type may also present problems to a group in the introductory phase of a cycle. Very likely, he'll be uncomfortable with the new ideas being discussed.

He won't poison the atmosphere, as might a resistance-testing-type, but he could be a strong negative influence if his opinion is valued and respected by the rest of the group.

If you're a leader with such a person in your group, you may be tempted to bypass him. But this would have a bad effect on the other members. They'd wonder if you'd treat them the same way, should they oppose group ideas or plans.

The best way to handle a termination phase-type group member is to find something for him to do in tune with his personality. He could be given the post of recording secretary, or he could be put in charge of the files, or given responsibility for work assignments. If you can keep him involved, it will have a good effect on the rest of the group, since he's likely to be one of its most stable members.

In the Simon family, Grandma Morgan—if she is to be included in the project—is the member most likely to fit this description, if only because she's in the termination phase of her life. To involve her and keep her active, Philip might ask her to keep a diary or scrapbook of the move. He could also give her other record-keeping tasks, such as making lists of the real estate offices visited and the houses seen.

It's possible, of course, that her mental or physical condition might not permit her to handle such jobs. In that case, Philip should do his best to keep her informed and involved, so that she is a supportive influence in the project, not suspicious and resentful.

Problems of Circumstance

Leader problems and member problems all have to do with the internal workings of a group. But the group is also affected by external matters, problems of circumstance.

All kinds of external events can affect a group, no matter what its phase. These can range from simple interruptions to severe crisis. They can include the death of the leader

The Introductory Phase

(or a member), new information that either simplifies or complicates the basic issue, or any other change in circumstances.

There's no time in the group process when these problems are more easily handled than in the introductory phase. At that point, no real changes have yet occurred. Unless the event takes place at the very end of the phase, no commitment to action has been made. The expenditure of resources has been modest.

Almost without exception, the group can handle such problems in its introductory phase merely by going back to the beginning, cranking in the new factor, then starting all over again. In the end, depending on content, the group might find it easier to reach a decision, or harder. Or, the new circumstance might so completely change matters that the idea is no longer valid, either because it's unnecessary or because it's impossible.

Let's say, for instance, that while the Simon family was discussing whether to live in the suburbs or the country, Philip got a raise, so the family realized it could afford a better house than they had thought. All the family would have to do is add that information to the original problem, then start the discussion over again, in essence.

Or, let's say that Grandma Morgan's health deteriorated to such an extent that she needed full-time nursing care, or she needed to be put in a nursing home. The financial drain on the family might then make moving out of the city impossible (or absolutely necessary, depending on its financial situation).

Whatever the change in circumstances, though, the solution is relatively simple: Begin the introductory phase again. And, since the group members probably wouldn't yet have a substantial emotional investment in the project, the group could probably take this in stride.

I repeat, the introductory phase can be very exciting. It's the time when your enthusiasm is high, when you're full of hope, when you're stimulated by a new idea or a new situation or a new circumstance, or by the formation of a new group. It is a time to let your ideas flow, a time for the group to feel the potential of the project.

The Resistance-Testing Phase

A Case History

Hank Starsky and Sara Stuart, both residents of a large, metropolitan city on the East Coast, first met in January, 1974, at a large, noisy party given by a mutual friend.

At the time, Sara was twenty-nine, a bright, attractive, small-statured woman with dark hair, hazel eyes, a ready wit, and a quick, nervous smile. A graduate of a local university, she was now head copywriter for the advertising department of a local chain of women's clothing stores, a job that paid her $14,500 a year.

Sara had been divorced three years earlier from Roger Stuart, an artist, who now lived in San Francisco and made his living selling cars. At the time of the divorce, Sara was awarded custody of the children (Jeff, eight, and Adam, four) and $100 a week in child support from Roger until she remarried, if ever. She and the children lived in a small downtown garden apartment near the job.

When he met Sara, Hank was forty-nine, a tall, distinguished-looking man with graying dark hair, blue eyes, and an aura of calm stability. A 1955 Dartmouth graduate, he was now the owner of a good-sized electrical supply house that had been in his family for years. He earned about $35,000 a year.

Hank had been widowed two years earlier, when his wife, Irene, died in an airplane accident. The marriage, which had been an unusually strong one, left him with two children, Mark, seventeen, a high school senior, and Doreen, fifteen, a sophomore in high school. Hank and his children lived in a large uptown luxury apartment, on the twenty-fifth floor of a forty-story building.

To escape the noise of the party and the unwelcome attentions of a young man in a plaid polyester knit suit, Sara had wiggled through the crowd of drinkers, eaters, and smokers and out onto the terrace, despite the chill. Hank was already there.

It took them only a few minutes to discover their mutual bonds: They hated noisy parties, they liked two-way conversation, they enjoyed good books, good movies, good music, and good food.

That night, Hank took Sara home.

What followed was a storybook courtship. Hank was an enormous change from the men Sara had been seeing. They'd been a mixed bag—some married, some disinterested in marriage, some exciting but unstable. Hank proved to be a thoroughgoing gentleman, a kind, considerate, caring man.

For Hank, Sara was like a breath of fresh air. He was charmed by her youth, her zest for living, her femininity. He'd gone out little since Irene had died, unable to imagine himself with another woman. But Sara made him feel young again.

The weeks that followed were filled with evenings at the theater, dinners, concerts, even a weekend ski trip. And it was on that ski trip, while the two of them sat huddled in front of a blazing fire at the ski lodge, that Hank proposed. Sara accepted quickly.

There were a few shadows in their relationship. Hank, after all, was twenty years older than Sara. And he was Jewish, while she was Catholic. Her children, both young, had taken to Hank easily. Hank's children, on the other hand, were friendly toward Sara, but reserved. In their romantic mood, however, none of these differences seemed very important.

On March 21, 1974, Hank and Sara were married in a small civil ceremony, attended by all four children, Sara's mother and father, and Hank's mother (his father had passed away eight years earlier).

With Sara's mother taking care of Sara's children and Hank's staying with their grandmother, the newlyweds then left for two weeks in Bermuda, where they had a glorious time.

When they came back, Sara and her kids moved into Hank's uptown apartment, which was large enough—barely —to accommodate all six of them. It meant getting up earlier for Sara, since it took longer to get to work, and it meant changing schools for her eight-year-old (the four-year-old stayed in the same nursery school).

All went well for the next couple of weeks. Hank and Sara were still in a honeymoon frame of mind. And the kids were taken with the novelty of their new situation. Then the trouble began.

Doreen, Hank's daughter, began complaining bitterly about Sara's children. She said they were always noisy, or always underfoot, or always wanting to play with her. She told her father she hated them. He told her she'd get used to the little ones and come to love them like brothers.

At about the same time, Mark, Hank's son, started having trouble in school. He'd never been that strong in math. Now he was failing, and working far below his abilities. After a note from the teacher, Hank told the boy he'd better settle down.

Meanwhile, Jeff began to fight with his younger brother continually. They'd had spats before, but nothing like the constant warfare they had now. Jeff told Sara that Adam "just bugs me all the time." Sara told Jeff that fighting was out.

A few days later, Hank and Sara had their first real argument. Hank suggested that she quit her job, stay home, take care of the kids, and "live a life of leisure, like Irene did." He understood, he said, why Sara needed to work before. But now that was unnecessary. He also said something about having a baby.

Sara was astonished and dismayed. She had a promising career and wanted to go as far as she could. She didn't think of herself as the housewife type. And she was surprised and disturbed to discover Hank's attitude on the subject. As for children, weren't four enough?

Hank was also disturbed, by Sara's attitude. He saw himself as a family provider. In his view, women weren't meant to work unless there was no man in the family. And, as for children, wasn't having them the essence of womanhood?

The argument was never resolved, just patched over. Hank turned on the charm and affection and Sara didn't have the heart, or desire, to turn him down. They wound up in bed.

It wasn't long after that Hank and Sara had his mother and her parents to dinner. The evening wasn't a success. All three parents managed to make snide remarks about the others' religion. The kids fought constantly, each turning to his or her own parent for support.

Later, Sara asked Hank to do some disciplining. But he insisted that keeping the kids under control was her job. He'd handle the spankings, but she had to set up the rules and enforce them. He was too busy to get involved, he said. Besides, riding herd on the kids was a mother's job.

Sara felt like telling Hank that she was busy, too, with her own work. But she'd always had trouble asserting herself in situations like this, so she said nothing. She did her best to get the kids to stop acting up, without much success.

Mark openly defied her, rarely doing his schoolwork, often staying out late. His grades continued to fall. Doreen spent the better part of most evenings on the phone with a boy she'd been forbidden to see (after he twice brought her home hours later than expected). Jeff and Adam continued to wage war on each other.

One night, after Hank and Sara went to dinner and the

theater, they returned home to find the apartment in a shambles. Mark and two buddies who shouldn't have been there had cleaned out the refrigerator, spilling beer everywhere. The little ones had painted the bathroom rug and were still awake. Doreen, who was supposed to be at home, had gone out with her boyfriend again.

Now Hank blew up, saying, "I won't let my children do this to me." He grounded Mark for a month. And, when Doreen got home, he did the same to her. To Sara's horror, he even spanked her kids, though they were only victims of poor supervision. To top things off, he yelled at Sara, saying the whole thing wouldn't have happened if she stayed home and acted like a mother should.

Sara didn't sleep that night (though Hank, as usual, dropped off a few seconds after his head hit the pillow). She couldn't stop thinking about what Hank kept saying about her job and her role in the family. She thought about the kids and how the marriage had turned all four of them into behavior problems. Wasn't everyone better off before the families had gotten together?

She looked over at Hank, sleeping beside her, her eyes filling with tears. True, she loved him, despite his antiquated attitudes toward women and his awkward way of dealing with children. But this whole thing just wasn't working out.

The next day, she sent Jeff and Adam to her parents' house and moved into a hotel until she could find a new apartment. Hank did his best to convince her to stay, saying things would get better, that they all just had to get used to each other. But Sara wouldn't be swayed. And they never did get back together again, so far as I know.

Resistance-Testing Phase LIFE-CONTROL

Could a knowledge of LIFE-CONTROL, or at least an instinctive understanding of process have saved this marriage? Let's take a closer look at what actually happened and see.

Looking back, it's clear that the marriage started off

with a clear-cut introductory phase, beginning when Hank and Sara met and culminating in their honeymoon. At that point, the amalgamation of their two families was still little more than an idea.

Then real change took place. The two families became one. Hank's children got a mother, Sara's got a father. Sara's family moved uptown, one of her children changed schools, and all three found themselves in close contact with three semi-strangers. Hank's family stayed put, but its routines and perspectives were drastically altered when Sara's family moved in.

Groups and individuals in families or other situations naturally prefer to keep doing things the way they've been doing them. The familiar pattern gives them a sense of security and stability, a confidence in their ability to predict events and therefore control them.

As a result, no group or individual welcomes change totally without reservation, even when that change is obviously pleasant, beneficial, or productive. Change diminishes feelings of security and stability. It reduces people's confidence in their ability to understand, anticipate and control events, either in the environment or within themselves, or both. It causes anxiety.

This anxiety doesn't usually show up until real change takes place, however. That's why Sara and Hank were able to enjoy their honeymoon and why their kids were able to feel enthusiastic about the marriage and the coming change in their lives. This was the introductory phase of the cycle, when it seemed to all that a union of the two families would solve most of their outstanding problems.

Then came the actual change, when Sara's family moved in with Hank's. With this change came anxiety. And with the anxiety came resistance to change, a normal, natural, predictable reaction to events, and the first major sign that a new phase had arrived. The honeymoon was over.

The resistance-testing that followed accounted for Doreen's objections to the smaller children, the sudden increase in fighting between those children, and Mark's falling grades.

It even accounted for Hank's behavior. When he told Sara she should quit her job and be a full-time mother, he was really saying, "I'd like this marriage to be like my other one." He was resisting change.

He was also testing Sara, pushing her to see if she would accommodate herself to his wishes, even though he knew she and Irene were different kinds of women, from different eras. Despite his pushing, however, he never told her that quitting her job was a condition of the marriage.

Even Sara was resistance-testing, though in a passive way. When she took over the disciplining of the children, she did so only with great resentment toward Hank, for not doing what she thought was *his* job. And her resentment made it difficult for her to handle the children effectively.

How long a group stays in resistance-testing—in fact, whether or not it survives the phase intact—depends on the sophistication and experience of the group's members and leadership. If everyone has been through similar situations before, resistance-testing may be brief. But that wasn't the case with the Starskys.

The length of resistance-testing also depends on how much of a change the group is undertaking. In general, the greater the change, the stronger the resistance-testing. The Starsky family underwent major change.

One way or another, a group will continue resistance-testing until it has regained its feelings of stability and security. If this turns out to be impossible, then the group either dissolves or remains stuck in resistance-testing, unable to go on to the productive phase. And this exactly describes the situation Hank and Sara faced.

Finding Stability in the Midst of Change

Clearly, there was no way the family could have gotten this sense of stability from its new circumstance. For everyone involved, the situation was unfamiliar, strange, and different—a sure source of anxiety, not security.

Instead, the family must get its feelings of stability and security from its leadership, Hank and Sara in this case. The same holds for any group. Members ask their leaders to prove that the leadership, at least, can handle the new situation and deal with the altered events that now make up the environment. They do this by testing the leadership in every conceivable way.

The Starsky family used its own particular content issues for this purpose. But the process issues they were grappling with were universal. The children were requesting reassurance from their parents that things were really under control. And Hank and Sara were asking for the same reassurance from each other.

At the same time the children, by acting up, were asking their parents for limits and guidelines. They wanted to know just how far they could go in this new environment. And Hank and Sara were asking the same question of each other.

Failing the Test

Unfortunately, neither leader passed the test.

The first thing Hank did wrong was to withdraw as a leader, at the moment the members of his group, his wife and children, were in the midst of resistance-testing. He tried to turn over the responsibility for handling these problems to Sara.

This put her in an impossible position. The only thing that could have ended the children's acting-up was reassurance and guidance from the entire leadership, Hank and Sara together. She couldn't be both father and mother.

Furthermore, Sara also needed reassurance and guidance from Hank. When he withdrew from the leadership, it made her feel even more insecure than before and set the stage for acting up on her part.

If Sara had understood what was going on, she could

have done much to set things aright by communicating her feelings to Hank. And, if he'd understood, he could have taken an active role in disciplining the children from the start.

Thus, either one might have taken action at this time that would have at least partially solved a major process problem. But neither understood what was happening. And, even if she had, Sara might not have been assertive enough to change Hank's mind.

The second thing Hank did wrong, when he finally did get involved, was to take the children's acting-up as a personal challenge and overreact to it by punishing them inappropriately in relation to their behavior.

He didn't realize that the testing a group puts its leader to is essentially impersonal. It may not look that way, since it's usually expressed in current content issues. But resistance-testing is part of the *process.*

If Hank had understood this, he would have reacted calmly but firmly. He would have passed the test by showing his kids that everything was under control, including his own temper. Instead, he demonstrated the reverse.

If Sara had understood the process and if she'd established good lines of communication to Hank, even in matters of conflict, she might have been able to take him aside and cool him off. She might have been able to give him enough emotional support to make him feel matters were well in hand.

But Sara was busy failing the children's test on her own. She failed to realize that their misbehavior was a request for guidance and direction. And, by not being sufficiently firm with them, she didn't give them the limits they needed in order to feel secure.

In a way, Sara was abdicating her leadership role, just as her husband had. If she'd had a better understanding of the process, she might have taken charge. But, as it was, she wasn't inclined toward assertiveness. And she displayed the same temperament when faced with resistance-testing and acting-up from Hank.

Like all resistance-testers, Hank was asking for reassurance and guidance. He wanted to feel that someone was in control (even himself). He wanted to know what new rules applied in this new situation. He wanted to find out what parameters described his new marriage.

Hank picked some very sensitive issues for resistance-testing, which is par for the course. Resistance-testing usually involves the most troublesome content problems in sight. They're a natural focus for anxiety.

Sara thought Hank was looking for *content* solutions to *content* problems. She thought he wanted to mold her to his will, to fit her into his housewife stereotype. Actually, he was looking for *process* solutions to *process* problems. He wanted guidance and reassurance.

Since she didn't understand, Sara mishandled Hank's resistance-testing. She argued with him briefly, then shut up, perhaps because she didn't want to make trouble, perhaps because she felt he wouldn't have stood for most opposition.

Whatever her reasons, she didn't provide the leadership he was requesting. She didn't set limits. She didn't do anything to help him understand the rules that governed this new marriage. If she had, things would have worked out very differently, I believe.

Instead, Sara had a fit of resistance-testing of her own. She walked out, an enormous overreaction to circumstances. And Hank let her go, though neither of them really wanted to see the relationship end.

If the two of them had understood the process issues they were dealing with, I think they could have solved their problems.

First, if Sara had realized what Hank was actually doing when he was asking her to give up her job, and she'd been willing to communicate her feelings, Hank probably would have accepted her stand. He would have taken her attitude as a "given" from then on.

Second, if she expressed her feelings about his sharing

the family leadership at all times, he probably would have responded favorably, especially if she were able to tell him why his cooperation and participation were vital.

Third, if Sara and Hank had communicated clearly to their children just what behavior was acceptable and what wasn't, punishing them appropriately, if necessary, the children very likely would have reverted to their normal level of misbehavior (considerably less than in this resistance-testing phase). They would have felt someone was in charge and was willing and able to enforce the rules.

And, once they'd cleared up the problems within the family, Hank and Sara—probably separately—would have been able to go to their parents and set some limits there, too, about what kind of religious remarks they'd tolerate and which they wouldn't.

What happened to Hank and Sara is a tragedy, especially since it need not have happened. Their fate and the fate of others like them is one of the reasons I decided to write LIFE-CONTROL.

Four Miniature Phases in Resistance-Testing

I chose the Starskys' case history to illustrate the resistance-testing phase, because I felt there'd be something in it for almost anyone to identify with. But I might just as well have described:

- The arrival of a computer in a business office and the resulting commotion among the employees;
- A change of managers on a baseball team;
- A transfer in which a company executive and his family move from one city to another, from one of the firm's offices to another;
- A divorce and its effect on both marital partners and their children; or
- A reorganization at work, in the army, in the country.

As with the introductory phase, and all the rest, it's the

process that is usually most important, not the content. And, to illustrate that process, I might have chosen any group, with any goal, as it confronted real change.

The resistance-testing phase, as you've no doubt guessed, is also divided into four parts. They may not be quite so clear as they are in the other phases, but they're still apparent. Here's how they looked for the Starsky family:

1. *The introductory part:* This began when Hank and Sara came back from their honeymoon and the families set up housekeeping together. It's when the negatives first started to show themselves, when the children started arguing among themselves, when the bloom was off the rose.

During this period, group members begin to realize that what was once a dream is now a reality; change has actually taken place. Whatever doubts, fears, frustrations, angry feelings, etc., they may have hidden during the excitement of the introductory now begin to surface. The change has made them anxious.

2. *The resistance-testing part:* In the Starsky family, this consisted of the arguments between the two sets of children, of Mark's falling grades at school, and of Hank's needling of Sara concerning her job and role.

During this period, the family wasn't really getting down to the main issue—whether or not the leadership, Hank and Sara, could restore its sense of security and stability. Instead, it was involved with peripheral issues, with side problems that appeared to have little process meaning.

3. *The productive part:* When the Starsky children finally started confronting the issues directly, they entered this segment of resistance-testing. Here, they were challenging the rules head-on, acting up on those issues that bothered them most, defying their parents.

It was at this time that Hank's needling of Sara took on serious overtones, that they began to argue and really confront one another.

During this part of the phase, group members stop talking about peripheral issues and second- and third-person complaints and begin discussing first-person problems. The process meaning of their acting-out, their need to be reassured and to have limits set, becomes clear at this point.

4. *The termination part:* For the Starsky family, this segment of the resistance-testing phase began when Sara packed up and left.

As the resistance-testing phase nears its end (although the end may seem nowhere in sight), it's very common for the group's testing and acting-up to spiral upward to a crescendo of troublemaking. Very likely, it will be worse near the end of the pattern than it was in the beginning.

This pattern is very common in individual therapy. Most experienced therapists learn to recognize it. It usually signals that the patient has absorbed what has gone before, that he's ready to move on, to make progress.

So it is with the group. This intense acting-up most often signals a growing strength in the group, an increasing ability to deal with the new situation.

If, at this moment, the leader demonstrates his ability to handle the new circumstance, to put events back into order, the group will usually respond quickly and well.

The Transition

In addition to the four miniature phases, the resistance-testing phase is sometimes marked by a fifth part, a transition between that phase and the productive phase.

This occurs when the group suddenly realizes that events are no longer out of order, that there is a reason to feel a renewed sense of security and stability. It's often marked by nostalgia, which is a way to put everything into perspective.

Of course, this doesn't always happen. Like the Starskys, many a group in the resistance-testing phase never gets out of it in one piece, or never gets out of it at all.

The resistance-testing phase contains more pitfalls than any other part of the cycle. If a group doesn't finish its task, it's usually because something went wrong at this stage in the process.

I've seen groups and individuals literally destroy themselves during the resistance-testing phase. It's not because their content problems were overwhelming. Usually, they were no worse than such problems are in the productive phase. It's because they didn't understand what was happening to them.

In the pages that follow, I intend to describe the various problems, both unique and general, that can turn the resistance-testing phase into a disaster. I'll explain why they happen, how to prevent them (when possible), and what to do about them if they happen anyhow.

What Can Go Wrong in Resistance-Testing

The problems unique to the resistance-testing phase mainly have to do with how the group's leader and its members handle the anxieties that inevitably accompany change.

Though these problems have a common core, and sometimes common causes and cures, they take at least four different forms. In order of increasing severity, they are: an attempt to avoid resistance-testing altogether; prolonged resistance-testing, in which the group never regains its stability; severe acting-up, even to the point of violence; and, finally, the group's abandonment of its original goals, or the dissolution of the group.

This is not just a list of problems, it is a progression. If a group with the first problem doesn't solve it, it will find itself with the second problem. And if it doesn't solve that, it will move to the third problem, and then to the fourth problem.

But let's take them one by one.

Trying to Avoid Resistance-Testing

Groups and their leaders both have a natural tendency to try to sidestep the conflicts inherent in resistance-testing, and move directly from the excitement of the introductory phase into the accomplishments of the productive phase.

The reasons for this tendency are clear enough: Resistance-testing very often isn't pleasant for either group members or their leader. For many, the phase's friction tends to increase anxiety, temporarily at any rate. The conflicts that appear evoke thoughts of serious struggle, failure, and dissolution of the group—and more instability and insecurity.

Many times, groups are so caught up in the pleasures and excitements of the introductory phase that the first hints of resistance-testing are very disturbing. It's as though the dream suddenly starts showing signs of turning into a nightmare.

And yet, it cannot be avoided, any more than a child can avoid adolescence and move directly into mature adulthood. In fact, the attempt to avoid resistance-testing complicates the phase, rather than making things easier.

When a big-city medical group I'm familiar with installed a small computer to handle billings and patient records, the office manager in charge of the change tried to avoid resistance-testing among the secretaries and nurses by announcing to one and all that modern times were here and that everyone was expected to cooperate. Objections were distinctly discouraged.

Superficially, everyone did cooperate. But trouble began almost as soon as the machine arrived. Billing mistakes, human errors in established procedures, quadrupled. The bookkeeper and the head secretary, never friendly, stopped speaking to each other. And a good young nurse quit.

This wouldn't have happened if the office manager had given those affected a chance to express their objections and doubts. Bringing a computer into the office meant major change and change inevitably causes anxiety. The office manager didn't let her subordinates discharge that anxiety.

Obviously, if the group never moves on through resistance-testing, it will never regain its sense of stability and security. It will never be able to move on to the productive stage. The group's goal will usually remain distant and unapproachable.

Eventually, when a group avoids resistance-testing long enough, the avoidance itself becomes resistance-testing. I know of an office supply house that was considering opening up a branch operation in the suburbs. A three-man committee was put in charge of finding a location, and they discussed alternatives for nearly six months without coming to a conclusion.

In this case, group members used an endless discussion of peripheral issues to express their anxieties about the coming change. After awhile, it was clear this discussion was actually a form of resistance-testing. They actually didn't want any change to take place. And they were testing the company president to see if he could demonstrate his control of the situation by moving them into productive-phase issues.

In some respects, this is the most difficult sort of resistance-testing to deal with. Since the main issues aren't being directly confronted and the group members aren't talking on a personal level, it's difficult to deal with the real problems, either on a process or a content level.

If you're the leader of a group that's behaving this way, you have a difficult job ahead of you. You must let the group members follow the natural path, from the peripheral to the personal. If you try to rush them, you may wind up locking them into their current behavior.

The solution to the problem of the office equipment supply house came not from the firm's president, as it happened, but from one of the committee members. He privately told his boss that the committee was getting nowhere and that some sort of deadline schedule was needed. In effect, this member became temporary group leader.

The president responded by telling the group to recommend ten sites within a month and narrow these down to three sites after another month. Given this structure and time limit, the committee moved ahead with no further problems.

It isn't easy for a member to exert his leadership capabilities during the resistance-testing phase. Usually, the leader will see a member's efforts in that direction either as a challenge to his leadership or as just more troublemaking. It's during the introductory phase that leaders are most receptive to members' ideas. Everyone is brainstorming then, not troublemaking.

In the case of the office equipment supply house, however, the leader didn't realize that the committee was resistance-testing (or, in his words, "dragging their feet"). When one of its members came to him to both describe the problem and suggest a solution, he was quite receptive.

If your group is dragging its feet, you'll eventually have to nudge them forward, past peripheral issues, past second- and third-person discussions, into personal confrontations on the matter at hand, or the group's goals will never be achieved.

One of the crucial factors here is time. If there's no urgency, no deadlines to be met, you might be content to let the group move slowly, at its own comfortable pace. But the longer the group takes to get down to business, the more distant its goals will become—and that goal must be worth accomplishing or the group wouldn't have committed itself to it.

If you wait too long, the group will become angry and frustrated, as it sees the goal getting no closer. This certainly would have happened to the office equipment supply house if nothing had been done. And the group probably would have directed some pretty vigorous testing at the company president, or felt very disenchanted with him, since he wasn't being a leader.

Eventually, therefore, you're going to have to put an end to the socializing and small talk in your group. You're going to have to urge the group to get on with it.

Without knowing the content your group is dealing with, there's no way I can tell you when to make your move.

There is a rule of thumb, however: Wait until you're fairly sure everyone in your group has gotten a chance to indulge in peripheral issues. Make sure no one is being stifled. Then make it clear it's time to move on.

It's a different problem entirely when it's the leader who's trying to avoid resistance-testing. That office equipment supply house president might simply have told his executives, "I've leased a building at 4537 Boynton Avenue in Hargrove. We're going to open a branch there next October. Now I want you all to get busy and draw up the necessary plans."

Group leaders do this mainly because they fear conflict. They may have been burned by previous frictions, they may not feel able to handle member objections, they may have no faith in the members' judgment or even in the goal or project at hand. They feel, for one reason or another, that conflict will either put their positions in jeopardy or threaten their groups.

The cure for this difficulty is at the core of LIFE-CONTROL. It's a matter of learning to see process, however it may be disguised in content, and to come to terms with the idea that resistance-testing is a necessary step in every group's progress toward its goal.

I'd like to say right here, before all of you start feeling guilty about your performances as leaders, that the tendency to try to skip resistance- testing is so common as to be standard operating procedure. Almost every leader, of almost every group, will try—at least initially—to avoid conflict. It's a natural and normal leadership response.

Part of the problem is that leaders—and members, too —look at the conflicts and frictions of resistance-testing as problems to be solved. That gives this part of the process an unnecessarily negative connotation, however. Even though I often find myself using the word "problem," I'd prefer to think of resistance-testing as an occurrence, not as a problem. And it's not something to be solved, but something to be experienced, to be handled, to move through.

When Resistance-Testing Goes on Too Long

Just as there are groups that try to avoid resistance-testing, there are also groups that unwittingly and unwillingly wallow in it, unable to move forward or backward. In these groups, the conflict is continual, though probably not highly intense all the time.

I know of a group in exactly this situation, a tenants' organization on Chicago's north side. This group was formed with the goal of getting the landlord to keep rent increases to a minimum, provide better building maintenance and security, and respond more quickly to complaints.

The first thing the group did, naturally, was to elect a president, then a vice president and secretary/treasurer. The next thing it did was to start discussing how it would achieve its aims.

A number of possibilities were suggested: petitions, face-to-face negotiations with the building owners, attempts to get newspaper or TV publicity, withholding rent, lawsuits, etc.

The group's president, a fair-minded fellow who didn't have a very forceful personality, made it clear to the group that they had to decide on their course of action by themselves. He would remain strictly neutral. He felt his job was to carry out their wishes, once they'd been expressed.

Instead of deciding on a course of action after a normal amount of resistance-testing, the group went into resistance-testing and stayed there. The battles between various group members were spectacular. Three lawsuit partisans quit the group and decided to take action by themselves. Two families began withholding rent without the others' approval. All attempts to get the president involved failed.

Resistance-testing, as I've said, is a way for group members to express their anxieties. It's also a way for them to ask that the leadership restore feelings of security and stability and provide intra-group behavior guidelines, so that the anxiety will subside and everyone will be able to start working toward the group's stated goal.

When the leadership does not respond, when it does not meet the testing directed toward it by the group members, when the group isn't reassured, it simply keeps on testing.

In this case it was a group member, the vice president, who finally resolved the situation. He suggested that the president be put in charge of operations and that he be put in charge of planning. The group was angry and desperate enough to agree.

It wasn't long before the vice president had demonstrated his capabilities. He instituted parliamentary rules of order into the meetings, cutting the bickering in half. He pushed through attendance rules that brought back those who'd quit earlier (the rules said nonmembers wouldn't benefit from group successes). He isolated a few of the least practical ideas and had them voted out of consideration.

By this time, the group realized it had a leader. It settled down quickly, voted to take steps in a progression—the least serious ones first, the more serious ones later (if initial efforts failed to budge the landlord). The last I heard from the group, it had accomplished its goals almost completely.

My point here is that groups (and individuals) will continue to test—act up, that is—until their requests for guidance are answered. Very often, this means setting limits of some sort, making it crystal clear what behavior is acceptable, what behavior is not, and what consequences an offender can expect.

The group may continue to test after that, but its purpose will be to see if the leader means what he's been saying, if he's willing to stand behind his words, if he's willing to act like a leader.

Once these doubts have been laid to rest, the group members will have the evidence of stability and control they've been seeking. The result will almost always be a sharp drop in acting-up and a readiness to move on to productivity.

Incidentally, in my view, this is why a policy of leniency in treating adolescent offenders may fail and a policy of guidance and direction may be more helpful. Judges feel that if they treat a delinquent gently, there's a good chance he will show gratitude and straighten out—and he might.

But an adolescent delinquent is in the resistance-testing period of his life, when he's undergoing enormous physical and emotional changes. If his troublesome acting-up is seen as testing, it's obvious that judicial leniency alone may not meet his needs.

Instead, the adolescent offender needs guidelines and limits. He needs to know there are some things he cannot do without suffering serious consequences.

Severe or Violent Acting-Up

All too often, what starts out as ordinary resistance-testing on the part of one or more group members turns into severe acting-up—defiance, very costly mistakes, sabotage of the group's goals, disloyalty, in-group rivalries or hatreds, even violence (directed at other group members, at the leadership, or outward).

Resistance-testing of this sort is no respecter of groups. It can happen in the family, on the work scene, in social clubs, in sports teams, in military units, in classrooms or schools, in ethnic groups, or any other task-oriented gathering.

An example of resistance-testing of this type occurred not long ago in a large automobile assembly plant in Pennsylvania. It all began with the installation of some automated equipment. No workers were fired or laid off, but many were reassigned to different, usually simpler jobs.

About a month after the new equipment began to function, the plant employees started resistance-testing. The absenteeism rate shot up noticeably, there was an increase in requests for transfer, and quality-control performance dropped.

The plant manager, a man who'd never worked through the resistance-testing problems in his personal life, came down hard on his employees. He sent out threatening memos, chewed out several workers while their colleagues watched, and talked about getting new automated equipment that would replace some workers.

The production employees reacted by acting up severely. Certain assembly operations were deliberately sabotaged, theft of parts skyrocketed, a foreman was seriously beaten, and two small fires "of suspicious origin" hit plant storage areas.

This sort of resistance-testing is definitely not par for the course. When I say that resistance-testing is a normal, inevitable part of the process that leads a group from a new idea to productive accomplishments, I'm not talking about conflict this intense.

Severe acting-up is most often caused by an overreaction on the part of leadership to normal resistance-testing. The leader who takes this part of the process as a personal challenge, and who lashes out angrily or defensively at those group members who are causing trouble, is inviting severe acting-up.

By resistance-testing, group members are essentially telling their leader, "I feel anxious and upset in the face of this change. I feel insecure. I want you to make me feel like we're in a stable situation again. And the way you can do that is by showing you're in command and control (especially of yourself) and can handle the changes we're experiencing."

But certain leaders will mishear the message. They'll interpret the group's acting-up as saying, "You're not a good leader. We know what to do better than you do. We don't have any respect for you. You can't tell us what to do."

These leaders don't realize that they're confronting a natural phenomenon, a part of the process that will go on no matter who's head of the group, no matter what the group thinks of its leader.

When the plant employees started to misbehave and act up, the plant manager misinterpreted what was going on. In part because of his personality and in part because of external pressures, he was so overcome by content that he was unable to see the process.

Instead of keeping his temper and responding appropriately, which doesn't necessarily mean leniently, he flew off the handle. He took the employees' behavior as a personal challenge. In effect he said, "I won't let you people do this to me." And he overreacted wildly.

His employees were testing him, true. But they were asking for more leadership, not less. They needed guidance and direction, not bluster and threat. They needed to know exactly what rules governed this new situation, not that the plant manager could be a dangerous man if crossed.

By overreacting to their test, the manager failed it and, incidentally, disobeyed the most basic precepts of LIFE-CONTROL. He did not give his men an increased sense of stability and security. If anything, they interpreted his behavior as a sign that he, too, was out of control, which he was. So their anxiety increased. They knocked again —louder.

If the plant manager had been able to look on his employees' resistance-testing not as a personal challenge but as a natural response to change, he probably would have been able to move the work force into production quickly. He should have made it clear that it would be business as usual, despite the new machines, but that his door was open if anyone had any problems to discuss.

Let's say that you're the leader of a group that's now in its resistance-testing phase. How should you handle the situation?

If the resistance-testing amounts to nothing more than disagreements with you or your policy, you'll probably do best not to challenge these contrary opinions. This will serve as an excellent demonstration of your self-confidence and leadership ability.

The opposite behavior, challenging or silencing every disagreement, will end up having the opposite effect

—revealing to your group (perhaps on an unconscious level) your weaknesses and insecurities.

If you permit differences and disagreements, your position will sooner or later be supported by members of your group. If you disallow them, they will flourish and grow stronger, like a muscle under tension.

If the resistance-testing progresses to the acting-up level, you will eventually have to take action, if only to show the members of your group that you have things under control and they can start doing some productive work.

But you should be careful to act, not to overreact. You should not get yourself into the bind of thinking you are being personally challenged or attacked. It will seem that way, from a content standpoint. However, that's the only way the process can reveal itself.

In this situation, I recommend a sort of "benign firmness," a cool, composed, controlled recitation and enforcement of the rules. You shouldn't be so firm that the slightest transgression calls for swift and decisive discipline, nor so relaxed that you end up forgiving even serious acting-up.

That's all well and good, you might say, but what if I've already overreacted? Is disaster inevitable? No, it's not.

When Bud Powers turned seventeen, he got his junior driver's license and got his father's permission to use the family station wagon at any time. His father, Harry Powers, set only four conditions:

First, Bud could never arrive home after dark (state laws prohibited those holding junior licenses from driving at night). Second, he could never return the car with an empty gas tank. Third, both his father and his mother had first call on the car. Fourth, he was to drive carefully and observe all traffic laws.

Bud faithfully followed these four conditions, for about ten days. Then he started to do some testing, a natural result of his changed circumstances from bike rider to car driver.

He twice got home after nine at night, both times with good excuses. He once brought the car home bone dry.

When reproached, he said he'd forgotten the family credit card. A few days later, Harry Powers noticed a deep gouge on the wagon's left front fender. Bud denied all responsibility.

The showdown finally came one Saturday morning, when Harry Powers started out to pick up some lumber for a tool shed he was building. He didn't get far. Bud had left with the car, even though his father had mentioned earlier that he intended to use it. Harry was furious.

When Bud got back around noon, his father asked him for his license, then ripped it up then and there. "You've got to learn that when I say something, I mean it," his father said. Bud protested that he'd expected to have the car back before his father needed it, but Harry Powers wasn't listening. He hopped into the car and started off toward the lumber yard, leaving his son on the curb, thunderstruck.

It's not hard to imagine what would have happened if Harry Powers had left matters that way. Bud would have been sullen and resentful. He might have taken the car without permission. He might have "borrowed" someone else's. One way or another, he would have continued to act up, probably severely.

But Harry Powers cooled off while driving to the lumber yard. He thought about what he'd done and decided he'd been wrong. As soon as he got home, he took his son aside, and practiced LIFE-CONTROL as if he were an expert.

First, he admitted he'd been wrong in tearing up the boy's license. He told Bud to tape it together again and, if that were impossible, immediately apply for a duplicate. He told Bud he was a good driver and he deserved that license.

By doing this, Harry was showing that he was concerned for his son's well-being and dignity. He was also demonstrating that he took his leadership role seriously and wanted to do his job well. And he was showing his self-confidence as a leader—exactly what he needed to do to make Bud feel more secure.

Second, Harry laid down the law. He made it clear that he meant the rules he'd set up and that he intended to enforce them without exception, from now on. For the next violation, he said, he'd ground Bud for three days. For the next, Bud wouldn't be allowed to drive for ten days.

This demonstrated Harry's leadership in another way, by showing that he was in control of the situation, after all, that he was willing and able to lead, to set rules and guidelines.

During this process, he managed to stand back a bit, taking care not to get himself back into a situation in which he could feel personally challenged or attacked. He looked at the whole picture. Perhaps he didn't consciously see himself as examining what was going on from the process point of view, but his actions demonstrated that's what he was doing.

Seeing events from the process viewpoint—I know, I've said it before, and I intend to say it again—is the key to LIFE-CONTROL. Its importance in confronting and dealing with your problems simply cannot be overestimated. After all, how can you handle a situation if you don't truly understand it?

When the Group Falls Apart or Gives Up

Bad things can happen to a group at nearly any point in the cycle. Even when things are going well, or apparently going well, there can be sudden breakdowns, swift descents into one kind of disaster or another. But there is no question that more bad things happen during a group's resistance-testing phase than at any other time.

More people get divorced during the resistance-testing phase of their marriages than during the other three phases put together. More workers are fired (or quit) during the resistance-testing phase of their employment than at other times. More children run away from home during the resistance-testing phase of their lives than before or after. More civil disturbances take place during the resistance-testing phase of national development than at other times.

Not long ago, for example, I had occasion to study tape recordings of a meeting of a college social activities committee. The school had appropriated thirty-five thousand dollars to sponsor some kind of student event. Just what that event was to be was the responsibility of the social committee. It was to consider the alternatives, make a selection, and draw up plans.

In the first part of the tape, there was the kind of discussion typical of an introductory phase. One person suggested a play. Another came out in favor of inviting a certain rock group to perform. Someone else wanted to have a dance. It was a typical discussion. There was no notable antagonism between the committee members.

All of a sudden, the leader—either impatient, or feeling challenged, or immersed in his own psychosocial problems—announced to the group that the discussion was over, that the committee was going to sponsor a concert by such-and-such rock group.

The group went into instant—and very fierce—resistance-testing. They attacked the idea from every possible angle. They tested the leader in every way they could think of. When someone else suggested that another group be invited, most of the members immediately agreed.

The leader, meanwhile, did his best to halt the debate. He made it crystal clear that he wasn't going to budge from his position, no matter what proportion of his group disagreed with him. And, when he was challenged, he took it as a personal attack. He invested so much of himself in his position that he was unable to abandon or modify it, however he might have felt about its merits on calm reflection.

Finally, his chief antagonist rose to address the group —and promptly resigned. He was quickly followed by the majority of the committee members. They quit, they said, because they were in favor of the other rock group. And maybe that's how they saw it at the time. But that was strictly a content explanation.

Actually, the group dissolved because the leader tried to move the group directly from the introductory phase to the productive phase, without allowing it to experience normal resistance-testing. He tried to dominate the group by sheer force of will, which proved impossible in this case.

In the end, the committee leader tried to get a new group together. But word of his manner of operation had spread. He was unable to form a new committee. As a result, there was no event; the thirty-five thousand dollars were never spent.

Later, I questioned a member of the original committee. "Was there really a strong difference of opinion about which group to invite?" I asked him.

"That's a funny thing," he told me. "Before the meeting started, I would have sworn that no one cared. Both groups were popular and well liked. After it was all over, I don't think anyone cared, either. I happen to know that some of the committee members who'd been very opposed to the group the leader suggested went to see them at a concert a few weeks later."

Obviously, this group could have gone either way. But, by his actions, the group leader threw it into vigorous and determined resistance-testing. He never came to see the error of his ways, so the group finally failed. And yet, it might have succeeded. The leader could have repaired his errors almost until the first member of the committee resigned, possibly even after that, by admitting his mistake and opening up the discussion again.

An alert member who understood LIFE-CONTROL might also have been able to alter the outcome (and temporarily assume leadership of the group, by the way). There were three opportunities:

The first—and best—came before the chairman arbitrarily made his decision, while the introductory phase was still in full swing: At that time, any member could have suggested that the group needed more information before it made any commitments.

He could have pointed out that to make a sensible decision the group needed to know what halls were available and on what dates, what performers could perform on the open nights, what the costs were, etc.

This suggestion would probably have resulted in the formation of a subcommittee to get the necessary information. And it might have satisfied the leader's need to avoid conflict and do something productive. Chances are, when the subcommittee reported back, the chairman would have encouraged intelligent, productive discussion of the alternatives.

The second opportunity, which was nowhere near as good as the first, came after the chairman of the group put his foot down, after resistance-testing blossomed. Here again, any member could have suggested that the group get more information. He could have volunteered his services in contacting the group the chairman favored and the groups favored by others.

So long as he made his suggestion seem like a productive idea, the member would have had a fair chance of getting the chairman to go along with it. And if the chairman said okay, that would have been a sufficient show of flexibility on his part to keep the rest of the group from backing out.

The third opportunity came after the group dissolved. Any member who wanted to could have re-formed the group, bringing in as many members of the original committee as possible, then gone to the administration, explained the situation, and asked to be given the responsibility for planning the event. If the member could have gotten a majority of the committee behind him, he probably could have carried it off and become the new group leader.

So, as you can see, failure and dissolution of this group was not inevitable.

Clearly, the proper behavior on the part of the leadership, or even from an insightful and determined member, can bring many a group through even very divisive resistance-testing to the relative safety of the productive phase.

But let's be realistic. That isn't always the case. Some people just can't get along together, no matter how skilled they are at LIFE-CONTROL. The basic chemistry is wrong.

When to Call it Quits

That leads us to another problem. If you're part of a group that looks like it's locked into resistance-testing—at home, on the job, among friends, or in any other group—how can you tell when it's time to give up all efforts at moving toward the goal, or even at keeping the group together, and let the inevitable take place?

Or, to put it more concretely, how can you tell when it's time to stop arguing with your spouse, stop struggling to please your boss, stop fighting with your "best friend," stop trying to get your club to go along with your ideas, stop trying to keep your bowling league together, stop battling your co-workers at every turn, etc., etc., etc., and get out?

This is a delicate, difficult problem, to which there can be no general resolution that will fit every situation. But there are some questions you can ask yourself that could help you make the decision.

• Is this continued resistance-testing in my group (or in my relationship with someone else or with several others) preventing me from becoming a productive person? Am I being held back by what's going on in the group?

• Is the resistance-testing in my group preventing me from developing myself professionally? Is my career being blocked by the conflicts I must deal with?

• Is this resistance-testing preventing me from living a happy and fulfilled life? Are my group relationships so sour that I can get no sense of satisfactions from the other things I do?

Depending on your frame of mind and the length of time your group has been in resistance-testing, it may be all too easy to answer "yes" to these questions, and terminate your ties to the group as a result. But before you quit your job or separate from your spouse, for instance, you should also ask yourself some tougher questions:

• Am I using the resistance-testing I'm experiencing on the job or in my marriage as an excuse for not developing or not working out my personal problems?
• Am I relying too heavily on my marriage or my job (or any other group) for satisfaction and fulfillment in life?
• Am I having the same kind of troubles in all of my groups, or have I always run into such situations?

To know when enough resistance-testing is enough, you must look at your entire life situation from a process viewpoint. You need the broadest possible perspective when you're making stay-or-leave decisions.

Problems That Can Happen at Any Time

Every group in the resistance-testing phase must somehow deal not only with problems unique to the phase, but also with the kinds of difficulties that aren't related to any phase, that can strike at any time—general problems.

These problems, as I pointed out in the last section, fall into three main categories: leadership problems, membership problems, and problems of circumstance. In this section, I will explain all three as they affect a group in resistance-testing.

Leader-Generated Problems

To be perfectly blunt about it, let me say that there is no other phase in which good leadership is as important as it is in resistance-testing. This is the time when group members are most in need of the guidance, direction, and sense of stability only a leader can provide. This fact naturally brings us to the first leadership problem.

When a leader isn't around. Whenever a group's leader cannot be with his group during resistance-testing, or whenever he withdraws from his leadership role, the immediate result is increased acting-up, more trouble.

Throughout their cycles, groups look to their leaders to make them feel things are under control. In the resistance-testing phase, this need turns into a demand. And it isn't enough for a leader to sit in his office, behind a closed door, taking those calls his secretary thinks are important enough. He must make his presence felt.

That's why wise school principals usually make it a point to walk the halls during the first few days of the school year, or whenever trouble threatens. They know that when the atmosphere of change or newness is strong, nothing has a more calming effect than visibility of the leader.

In a sense, the principal who walks the halls in times of school unrest is showing the flag. He's making it clear to all that they have a leader and that he's ready to act, if necessary.

The boss who occasionally stops in at his employee's office and asks, "How are things going?" is doing the same thing. He's not seeking an answer, really, but merely trying to show he's there to help. So is the maître'd who visits each table in his restaurant and asks if everything is satisfactory.

Yet, there are times during a group's resistance-testing phase when a leader cannot be present. Other business, other problems, other work may take him away from his group. He may even go on vacation, if he isn't aware of what effect that might have on group members.

There are also times when a leader might purposely withdraw, because he cannot handle the demands being put on him, or out of anger or pique, or to give an underling a chance to show his stuff, or for any number of other reasons.

Without a leader, the group in resistance-testing becomes more anxious than before. It acts up more than ever. Group members tend to pair off with one another, either to fight and argue or to get involved in peripheral discussions that do nothing to advance the group toward its goal.

I personally witnessed a good example of what happens when a leader withdraws during resistance-testing. It occurred when I was chief of pediatrics at an army hospital.

At the time, I had two pediatricians working for me. One was a regular army type, a career soldier. The other was a civilian doctor who was serving out his enlistment. He intended to go back to civilian practice when he got out of the army.

The regular army doctor handled his young patients very well from a medical standpoint, and very efficiently. And, at the end of each appointment, he'd tell his patient's parents that he wanted to see the youngster again in ten days for a follow-up, but indicated that he did not expect to hear from them until then.

The civilian-oriented pediatrician was an equally good and equally efficient doctor. However, he told the parents that they should feel free to call on him at any time if there was any difficulty or problem. He also asked that they bring in their children after ten days, for a follow-up.

What happened then was fascinating. The regular army doctor had virtually no repeat visits or telephone calls from the parents of his patients. But the after-hours emergency room was literally filled with his patients, day after day.

The civilian-type doctor, who'd told the parents that he was available if need be, had a few calls, not many. But not one of his young patients showed up in the emergency room.

When you think about the principles of LIFE-CONTROL, it becomes quite clear why this happened. The parents who brought their sick children to the army-type doctor were anxious and worried. They wanted someone to take the leadership role in this situation and remain active until there was nothing to worry about.

By cutting off communications, the army-type doctor failed to provide the reassurance the parents needed. Their anxiety level remained high. On the other hand, the parents who saw the more flexible physician were given the feeling that a leader was on the scene and available. Their anxiety diminished.

If you're a leader, I'm sure I don't have to tell you now that it's a LIFE-CONTROL precept to stay close to your group when it's in the resistance-testing phase and to be as visible as possible.

But there may be times when you cannot help being absent. And your group may have so many problems that you cannot deal with them all personally or you'll never get your own work done. What can you do in those cases when you must be absent or you must temporarily withdraw?

Even when you delegate authority clearly and wisely, it's not the same as if you were still on the scene. This is especially true in the case of a particularly strong leader or a particularly weak or little-known right-hand man. The group's anxieties and discomfort will almost certainly increase, though not to the level they'd go if there were a total vacuum at the top.

LIFE-CONTROL theory provides one very good way a temporary, delegated leader can keep things under control, should he find himself in charge of a group in the resistance-testing phase:

The more a leader can verbalize the discomfort that a group feels, the less the group members will have to act out that feeling.

In other words, the temporary leader can discuss the group's anxieties and encourage the group to discuss them, letting them be discharged by words instead of deeds.

Substitute teachers do this all the time. They settle down their classes quickly by talking about the absent teacher— how much the children miss her, what routines she followed, when she'll be back, why she's gone, etc.

All of this accomplishes that most desirable end: It increases group security. It gives members—students, in this case—a feeling that everything is under control. It lets them turn away from their worries and start considering their work.

If the leader is going to be unavailable for only a short

time, the temporary leader can handle minor problems and postpone the major ones until the big boss gets back. Many a mother does this daily when she tells her children, "Let's wait until your father gets home. We'll discuss it then."

In the end, however, there is simply no substitute for leader presence during the resistance-testing stage. That's why Russell Oswald couldn't end the prisoner rebellion at Attica. Governer Rockefeller, the true leader, was the only person who would have given the group a sense of stability and security.

The wise leader won't leave his group at all during the resistance-testing phase. He'll schedule his vacation for some other time. He'll put off other work so he can involve himself with the group actively and continually.

Blame yourself first. When something goes wrong, everyone's inclination is to find someone else to blame. Group leaders also exhibit this human frailty. Especially during resistance-testing, when problems and difficulties abound, they tend to carefully examine members of the group to see who's doing what wrong and why. This kind of behavior, however, builds anger and resentment among group members.

Let's say you're the manager of a bank branch in a big city. To clear up those long lines of customers that queue up in front of the tellers' windows at lunch hour every day, you devise a new waiting system, in which customers are greeted at the door, asked about the type of transaction they're making, then directed to teller "specialists."

Soon after you put the new setup into effect, things begin to go wrong. One of your tellers keeps coming down with minor, unexplained illnesses. Another draws angry complaints from customers about how slow she is. A third is observed being openly rude to a customer. As a result, the lunch-hour lines grow longer and longer. What do you do now?

Your natural inclination would probably be to identify those employees who aren't performing properly and ask them to come into your office for a serious personal chat.

But, if you do that, you may be missing the main source of your problem. About 50 percent of the time, from what I've found by studying groups of all kinds, the problem lies more with the leader than with the members.

It may be that you haven't clearly explained what you were doing and why. Or, it may be that your idea is no good; that, for example, your branch gets far more people making withdrawals than deposits, so the "deposit specialist" teller has too little to do.

It may be that you haven't considered alternate plans, such as the one-line-many-tellers-approach that funnels waiting customers to the first available window. Or, you may not have been involved enough when the plan went into effect and thereby missed some of the problems that arose, and continued.

At any rate, if you get yourself into a situation like this, the first thing for you to do is to see how you're contributing to the problem. It may be, of course, that you've performed flawlessly, that your idea was perfect in every respect, and that you followed the precepts of LIFE-CONTROL at every turn when introducing the innovation. It is true, I admit, that 50 percent of the time whatever has gone wrong *isn't* the leader's fault.

If that's the case here, your second step is to look at the system by which the group operates, and still not at the individual member. Examine each part of the organization individually and as it relates to the other parts.

You may be working with a format in which important tasks have been left unassigned. For example, no attempt may have been made to explain the new queueing system to the customers. Or, you may find that one job depends on another, but the wrong one is done first. For example, the person assigned to teach the "greeters" may not have been well briefed himself. Or, you may find there are enormous communication gaps between yourself and your employees, that your changes look like promotions and demotions, for example.

It may be that you haven't anticipated the problems of

success. Your system may be so good that it gets overloaded with customers who'd formerly banked at other branches, for instance. Or, the operations of your group may not mesh with the operations of other groups with which it must interact. Your plan may conflict with the plans of the head office.

But let's say that none of these things is true. Let's say you find you're working with a perfectly valid system. (And you may know it's valid, because the identical system seems to be working well for other groups.) Your group should be going into the productive phase by now, but it isn't. Why?

The third and final place to look for the answer is at the individual members of the group. You may find you have mismatched jobs and people, putting a teller who enjoys working out complicated transactions, for example, in the quick-deposit window.

You may find that certain members don't have the skills they need to perform properly. In our example, you may discover that one of your tellers needs a break every fifteen or twenty minutes and can't handle a steady stream of customers. You may discover that some members need special attention and care, that they have exceptionally high anxiety levels.

The again, you may discover that one member of your group is an antisocial personality, who's dividing the rest of the members, perhaps leading them in a direction opposite to the stated goal. Such people characteristically like to polarize their groups, then sit back and watch the group members act out their (the antisocial person's) anger.

For example, one of your tellers may be a very political sort, someone who's constantly worried about being exploited or forced to carry more than his share of the load. He may see your plan as a scheme designed to take advantage of him and the other tellers, and do his best to disrupt it and lead his colleagues in a rebellion.

The solution to most of these problems will become obvious just as soon as you have identified them. As for the antisocial type, however, you're going to have to either get rid of him, isolate him from the rest of the group, or work very closely with him.

To recap: When your group has problems and you're the leader, start looking for causes (and solutions) first by examining your own actions, second by studying the organization, and third by taking a closer look at the individual group members.

At this point, you may be wondering just why I've spelled out in such detail a formula for tracking down the cause of your group's problems. There are two reasons. First, I'm trying to provide you with a *modus operandi* for problem-solving, a technique you can use in any phase. Second, I'm trying to show you a way you can avoid the resistance-testing phase's worst temptation, overreaction.

When a leader lacks confidence. In my discussion of the introductory phase, I said that to be effective a leader must make the group feel he's capable of handling whatever comes along. This is especially true during the resistance-testing phase, when a group's anxieties are at their peak.

However, just because a leader lacks confidence, or is fragile or weak, doesn't mean he'll be tested more vigorously by the group than a strong leader. In fact, the reverse is often true.

Because of its need for leadership and its basic respect for the position, a group is likely to treat its leader with caution and care if he's fragile. If one group member attacks him vigorously, the others will usually come quickly to his aid.

But groups have little compunction about testing a strong and capable leader. In fact, the more capable a leader seems, the more frequently and vigorously he's likely to be tested. The group will demand more of him in the way of providing security and a sense of control precisely because he's more able to meet their demands.

We've seen this phenomenon in many big city school systems lately. Weak, comparatively ineffective leaders— administrators, principals, etc.—were tested only mildly by the community. Very often, there was little community participation in school affairs at all, positive or negative.

Then, new and stronger administrators came on the scene and invited the community to participate. Instead of acceptance and support, they received the pent-up anger, frustration, and resentment that had been building up for years, feelings the community hadn't felt able to share with the weaker leader.

The problem with a weak leader is that he usually cannot provide the members with a sense of security. Therefore, the anxiety generated by change remains undischarged. Groups in this situation progress slowly toward their goals if at all, usually spending long periods in low-level resistance testing.

If you're a leader who suffers from lack of confidence and your group is in the resistance-testing phase, there are some LIFE-CONTROL techniques that should make your situation more bearable.

First, become more expert concerning the content your group is working with. Knowing all you need to know—and more—can't help but make you feel more confident, since it will increase your self-esteem. It will also increase the esteem in which the group holds you, thus affirming your leadership position.

Second, get expert help or advice. Someone in the group may know more about one or more aspects of the task than you do, perhaps through experience. Go to him for help and advice. If he has broad knowledge and has good general capabilities, consider making him your right-hand man. Many an army captain has been saved by the wise guidance of his top sergeant.

Third, share the responsibility, either with that right-hand man or with the rest of the group. Follow democratic forms—voting, rules of order, etc. But don't fade into the woodwork. Remember, the group needs a leader.

Fourth, create a structure or plan of attack. Very often, an idea, intangible as it is, can assume a leadership role.

During the Watergate affair, for example, the country's leadership role was held not so much by President Nixon as by the Constitution.

From everything I've learned about groups and leaders over the years, it's become clear to me that leadership is a matter of how someone acts, not what someone knows.

Let me give you an example out of my own experience. A couple of years ago, a psychiatric resident at Johns Hopkins Hospital called me up and said he was having trouble with a man who'd been brought into the emergency room, evidently against his will.

When I got there, I saw a big husky man who was obviously very paranoid. He was angry, anxious, ready to explode. Whenever anyone approached him, he tensed up as if getting ready to lash out. I admit it, I was scared of him.

I took one look at him and walked out of the room. "Get me the biggest orderly on the staff," I told the resident. He found me three big attendants. Then I walked back into the room, with the orderlies close behind.

"How are you?" I asked, sticking my hand out to be shaken. "You must be scared as hell."

The guy looked at me, blinked, took my hand and shook it vigorously, as if he were holding on for dear life. Before long, he was completely calmed down.

Two things happened here worth noting. First, I examined my own feelings. I knew I couldn't go in there alone. I wouldn't have any self-confidence. And if I'd tried to fake it, he would have picked it up immediately. So I got myself some reinforcements. When I finally did go in, I *knew* I could handle the situation, with help.

Second, I showed him that I was in control of the situation. That's what he was asking for by his anger and fear. He was showing me how troubled he was and how much he needed help. When I was able to give him the feeling of security he needed, he settled right down.

It wouldn't surprise me if you're now saying to yourself, "It wasn't Glass who made the guy quiet down, it was those three monster orderlies." Not true, and I have another example to prove it.

One of my colleagues, a psychiatrist at the psychiatric ward of the Henry Phipps Clinic at Johns Hopkins, got involved in a similar situation. He was off duty when the whole thing began.

It started when a huge emotionally disturbed man (6'4", 260 lbs.) started threatening the staff members. They barely managed to lock the ward door against him, and immediately called my colleague.

When he arrived on the scene, he told all the staff members to follow him closely, to back him up. Then he unbolted the door and walked right into the room.

"I want you to stop this nonsense!" he told the patient firmly.

There was a moment's hesitation. Then the patient responded. "Yes, sir," he said, "I'll behave." And he went back to his room.

My colleague turned to see how the staff members had reacted to his masterful handling of the scene to find that he was completely alone. Not one staff member had had the courage to accompany him.

Obviously, the physician, who was much smaller than the patient, had conveyed a feeling of control. He had enough self-confidence—based on a false assumption, it's true—to convince the patient he could handle whatever might happen.

This physician, like myself in my situation, hadn't felt enough self-confidence to go in without help. But with help, or the impression of help, everything was fine.

Some talented leaders have enough self-confidence not to see a test as a test (or as a problem). In fact, they often find a way to use the energy produced by resistance-testing in some productive manner. They see the positives, not the negatives. Under this kind of leadership, group members quickly calm down and start producing. They know they're in the hands of someone who can keep events under control.

There is such a thing as a too-strong leader in resistance-testing, however. Leaders who are too capable, too charismatic, too self-confident, frequently force members to bottle up natural feelings of doubt or anxiety.

These feelings must come out eventually. When they do, they often get displaced to someone else in the group, a scapegoat. These usually innocent individuals must bear the anger or concern the group members feel toward the leader.

This is nothing more or less than indirect resistance-testing. Trouble over the scapegoat distracts the group from its main goal, and presents the leader with a problem that must be solved if the group is to get untracked.

If you're this kind of leader, you'd do better to allow the members of your group to express their doubts and anxieties directly, by eliciting criticism (if it isn't forthcoming), by making it absolutely clear that you welcome opinions and feelngs, even if they differ from your own.

If you don't do this, if you permit the group to find a scapegoat, you're making trouble for everyone. When anxieties can't be directly expressed and dealt with, they linger. The group stays in resistance-testing. Even worse, perhaps, you may lose the services of the scapegoat, a potentially productive member of the group.

When the leader is out of phase. If in its resistance-testing phase, the group finds itself with a leader who inspires confidence, who's willing to let the group members test him without overreacting, who knows when and how to exert his authority, it can hardly ask for more.

During the Great Depression, a kind of national (even international) resistance-testing phase, the United States was lucky enough to have such a man at its helm, Franklin Roosevelt. His predecessor, Herbert Hoover, a good and capable man, was basically a productive personality. When the depression hit, he found himself out of phase with the country.

Groups can just as easily find themselves with leaders who aren't suited to the rigors of resistance-testing, either by reason of personality or because of life circumstance, as they can with the right person at the right moment.

A group in resistance-testing might, for example, find itself with a leader who's basically an introductory phase-type, a man disinclined to institute rules and regulations or to enforce them, someone who likes things loose, not controlled, someone whose main concern is ideas rather than routine.

In an advertising agency, for instance, writers and art directors come up with commercials. They're introductory phase people. But account executives are called in to sell the ideas to clients. The account executives are experts at handling resistance-testing.

Or, a group in resistance-testing might find itself with a productive phase-type, a person who has little patience for dissension, even when it serves a purpose, someone who wants nothing more than to get on with the work. His inclination would be to try to solve problems on a content basis, logically and reasonably. He probably wouldn't realize that the group was going through a necessary stage on the way to production.

The almost prototypical production phase leader is the basketball coach or football manager, particularly on the professional level. He wants to win. That's what production means, so far as he's concerned. He's not likely to be sympathetic when his players act up, whatever their reason.

Or, a group that's in resistance-testing might find itself with a termination phase-type, someone who's more interested in the past than the present, someone who enjoys looking backward. He'll want to tidy up and put things in order. The cacophony of resistance-testing will upset him deeply and he may not want to recognize it for what it is.

In some ways, Dwight Eisenhower was a termination-phase president, and in a termination-phase era. It was that moment in history just before the space age, the beginnings of the civil rights movement, the population boom, the explosion of suburbs, and the Vietnam War, etc.

If you're a member of a group in resistance-testing whose leader is out of phase, what can you do? I've already discussed this in the introductory phase chapter, but let me review the appropriate LIFE-CONTROL principles briefly. You and the other group members, working together or singly, can:

1. Try to ease the leader into resistance-testing by setting up a suitable structure, or by taking the smallest possible steps forward;
2. Attempt to convince him to step aside temporarily and delegate the leadership; or
3. Divide responsibilities according to the phase personalities of the group members.

In each of these cases, of course, you and the other group members will be exercising part of the leadership, since you'll be helping to guide the group through resistance-testing. This will be a very difficult task if you don't understand LIFE-CONTROL, at least instinctively. The leader may fight you all the way.

If you're a leader who's out of phase with his group, you have three main alternatives: You can learn to be more flexible, to adjust to the flow of the process; allow or appoint someone else to take over temporarily, until the phase(s) you're best able to handle come up; or relinquish your leadership altogether.

Member Problems

For the most part, the member problems a group is likely to face in the resistance-testing phase are the same ones I talked about in the section on the introductory phase and are handled the same way. These include low skill levels, isolation, and "elopement."

The problems a group may have with out-of-phase members, however, require their own particular treatment during resistance-testing. And there's one more to worry about from here on in, the antisocial group member. Let's start with him.

Antisocial members. Resistance-testing may be a necessary and inevitable part of any group's progression toward its goal, but it can be unnecessarily lengthened and exacerbated by an antisocial individual, someone who has a great deal of inner anger and fear.

Antisocial people are the ones with chips on their shoulders, the ones who are always saying, "Let's you and him fight." They're troublemakers who seem to enjoy disorder.

You'll know the antisocial person in your group because he'll be the one who encourages your members to split up into opposing factions. To accomplish this, he may take one position on one occasion and another on another. When someone attempts to finds grounds for a compromise, he may identify areas of difference. When someone tries to cool tempers, he may try to fan the flame.

The antisocial person may actually make trouble himself, or he may encourage others to make trouble. Oftentimes, he's like a movie director who gets others to act out his fantasies. Only his fantasies have nothing to do with entertainment. They're all about disruption and disorder.

What can you do with such a person? To some extent, it depends on the type of group you're involved in and what content it's dealing with. In the family, for instance, the antisocial member must be helped if at all possible. His personal thought-system problems must be dealt with, perhaps professionally. On the job, however, the leader's best course of action may be simply to fire the man.

Actually, there are many different things you can do with an antisocial member.

- You can take him aside and try to show him the error of his ways. This may work if his problem is a minor one, and if you can devise an appropriate reward or punishment to motivate him.
- You can shunt him aside, into a harmless job that takes him out of the main flow of events and away from the rest of the membership.
- You can ignore him. But there are dangers here. If he's seeking attention, ignoring him will only make him redouble his efforts.

- You can pair him off with his opposite number. It may be possible to find a calm, steady, level-headed partner for the man, perhaps one who can guide him into productive behavior. But this requires care, too. There's always the chance that you'll get the opposite result, and lose one of the most valuable members of your group.
- You can get rid of him. If you have an unrecalcitrant sociopath in your group, this may be the only real answer to your problems. This is especially true of the man who wields a great deal of influence among the other group members, perhaps because he has a charismatic personality.

It's tricky to drop a group member (or even to punish one severely) without adversely affecting the whole group. If you are hasty or arbitrary, if the punishment does not fit the misdeed, morale may drop because the rest of the group may assume it can expect the same treatment after misbehaving.

On the other hand, if you're hesitant or lenient, morale will drop because the group may feel the situation isn't firmly under control. It may think you don't really have the ability to deal with the recalcitrant person.

If you act appropriately—justly and at the right moment—the group will probably be relieved. On a gut level, it will have sensed that it could never attain its goal while a fellow member was dividing everyone. Once he's gone, a great deal of tension and anger will vanish with him.

Furthermore, your discipline of the sociopath (or anyone else) will help other group members toward an internal sense of security and stability. They take your actions as guidance and direction. It will help them know what they can—and cannot—do. It will help you control the group.

Out-of-phase members. You might think that a member who's out of phase when the group is in resistance-testing, one who's either in the introductory phase, the productive phase, or the termination phase, will be someone you don't

have to worry about, since he won't be giving you problems.
Not so.

The man who's essentially an introductory phase personality, because of what's going on in his personal thought system or because of his life phase, may give you as many problems in resistance-testing as anyone else.

At precisely the moment you want to get your group moving on the idea to which it's committed itself, he'll be full of new ideas or disturbing modifications of the old idea. In effect, he'll be resistance-testing, but in his own peculiar manner.

Let's say you're building yourself a vacation house in the mountains. You've had an architect design the place and you've found a contractor. After weeks of haggling over prices and dates, you're all set to go. Then your architect shows up one night at your doorstep, with some "terrific" new ideas.

If you let yourself and the contractor examine all of his new ideas in detail, your vacation house may not be ready for occupancy until the middle of the next decade. You may even find yourself back in the introductory phase: trying to decide which is best, the original idea (the one to which you and your group had committed itself to) or the new idea.

One way to handle this is to let the man speak his piece. Look at his plans. Then let him know that enough is enough. If he doesn't get a chance to say what's on his mind, he'll probably disrupt the group again and again, until the last brick is in place. So give him a fair hearing.

Another way to handle this man is to look at his assets rather than concentrating on his liabilities. Find some part of the task in which his steady output of new ideas will be valuable. Ask him to come up with alternate ways of doing parts of the job that still aren't settled. In the case of the architect, you might talk to him about built-in furniture, or about future additions.

When you find yourself with such a man, put him in charge of making plans, or coming up with names and titles, or developing new projects. Remember, he's an idea man. Find some area where ideas are sorely needed and hand it over to him.

The man with a productive-phase personality won't be an out-and-out troublemaker, most likely. What trouble he makes will show up mainly as impatience to get on with the job. Your main problem with this man is how to hold onto him, a problem I discussed in the introductory phase section.

Let's say that you've gotten that vacation house built, finally, and you've invited a dozen friends over, in hopes of having it painted inside and out before the rain comes. And rain is predicted for tomorrow.

But for the first hour they're there, all your friends do is argue about who's going to paint where and who'll go out for the hamburgers at lunchtime and who's going to be the first to visit.

One fellow, a quiet type and a hard worker, is starting to get disgusted. You may lose him if the nonsense continues. He's a no-nonsense guy. What do you do?

Remember, the production-phase personality is basically a person who wants and needs to get to work. The best thing you can do is put person and work together. Perhaps you can give your hard-working friend some setting-up tasks— taping the windows, stirring the paint, spreading paper on the floors, etc. Maybe you can split off part of the work from the main project and put him in charge of it; give him the garage, for instance.

Whatever you do, it's essential to be sensitive to this person's needs. If you overlook them, you could lose someone who's potentially among the most useful members of the group.

The termination-phase personality could turn out to be either a substantial asset or a substantial liability during your group's resistance-testing phase, depending in part on the ages, interest, backgrounds, and personalities of the group members.

Let's say you're the breadwinner in a family that consists of two teen-aged children—both in resistance-testing—yourself, and your eighty-four-year-old mother. The kids spend most of their waking hours acting up and driving you up the wall.

Depending on her personality, Grandma may be able to help. She may be able to recall to her grandchildren her own youth, empathizing with them sufficiently to capture their interest and imagination, but giving them a perspective on life they'd never be able to see by themselves. It might calm them down a bit.

Or, take the same cast of characters again, but with a fearful old woman as Grandma, rather than someone able to share some of the wisdom she's gained. In that case, she might show her horror at what children do nowadays, thus earning not their respect but their contempt.

They'll see her as an old fuddy-duddy and she'll see them as part of a new order of semihumans. This could further complicate your problems, since the group would not only be in resistance-testing but also divided against itself.

How can you tell? Well, you'll never know if you don't ask yourself these questions:

Where do each of the members in my group stand? Who's in what phase, if any? Who's moving from one phase to another and who's stuck?

What are their needs? Do they want to get to work? Do they want to sit around and blab, afraid of getting down to business? Do they want to reminisce?

What are their assets and liabilities? Who can hurt the group by his behavior—and how? Who can help—and how?

How do they relate to one another? Are any members of your group in natural conflict because of their differing phases? Do any pair off naturally, either to the group's detriment or in some positive way?

Once you've asked—and answered—these questions, your proper course of action will be clear to you in most cases. You'll know whether to keep the termination-phase man in the thick of things, so you can take advantage of his stabilizing influence, or to find some task suited to his talents and interests that removes him from the scene of conflict and helps limit resistance-testing.

Most members in your group, in any group, won't have "pure" phase personalities of any one type. They'll be mixtures. But the tendencies toward a particular phase may dominate their personalities. If you're aware of this, you can treat them in a manner that will give them an opportunity to meet their needs, while providing the group with its best chance for success.

When circumstance intervenes. What happens to a group in the resistance-testing phase when something unexpected happens, anything from a simple interruption to a serious crisis?

To some extent, this will depend on the nature of the circumstance. If it involves major change—a shift in goals, a new leadership, a massive alteration in the group membership—chances are that the group will regress all the way back to the introductory phase. New commitments will be needed from the membership before the group can move forward again.

To cite a recent example, when Nixon suddenly left office and Ford became President, the nation and its new leader found themselves in an introductory phase-type of relationship, and a "honeymoon" began.

Lesser changes, however, such as relatively minor modifications of the original goal, the addition (or subtraction) of a group member or two, a change of locations, and so on, will tend to extend or intensify resistance-testing, usually in direct proportion to the extent of the change.

The same holds for smaller groups. I know of a junior high school in a rough big-city neighborhood that had been in resistance-testing for two years. The principal hadn't been able to find a way to cure the rash of behavior problems, truancy, low academic achievement scores, etc.

Then the new school, a replacement for the old building, opened up one fall. For the first two months, the principal told me, he felt like he'd switched student bodies with some rural junior high in Montana. Behavior was just about perfect.

What had happened was that the student body had gone back into the introductory phase. I'm sorry to report that it didn't last. They followed the pattern and were soon resistance-testing again. But the vacation from trouble had given the principal a new perspective and he handled the situation far more calmly than before.

The resistance-testing phase is often one of turbulence and increased anxiety. People don't want to change. But it isn't the end of the world. It doesn't mean collapse is imminent and inevitable. (It can even be fun. Many couples seem to enjoy their spats when they're in the resistance-testing phase of their marriage.) Resistance-testing is just another natural part of the process, something to be lived through, and experienced on the road to the productive phase.

The Productive Phase

A Case History

When Ed Savino married Judy O'Horban in June, 1960, she was twenty-four, an assistant buyer with a large, metropolitan discount department store. He was twenty-six and a junior executive with a major manufacturer of over-the-counter medicines. They'd met about a year earlier at the wedding of mutual friends.

They had an idyllic honeymoon in Jamaica. When they returned, they talked about beginning a family and decided they really wanted a couple of kids.

Within three months of their own wedding day, Judy got pregnant. Before their first anniversary, their first child, Rodney, was born and Judy had quit her job to be a full-time mother and housewife. A second child, Marcia, followed a year later.

Those first few years weren't easy ones for the Savinos. Ed was barely making enough money to support a family. Both found it difficult to make the adjustment to married life after several carefree years as young singles. Judy missed her job and the stimulation of the people with whom she'd worked. Then there was the problem of Ed's mother, who was in and out of the hospital—never for anything serious—and who phoned and visited her son with intrusive regularity.

Just before their fourth anniversary, things got so bad that Judy took the kids and went to a residential hotel. But their friends got them back together, to their mutual relief.

By the time the kids were in school, Ed had moved far enough up the promotional ladder that they were able to relax their strict budget a bit. Judy had settled down and was playing the housewife's traditional role, participating in parent-teacher associations, taking charge of entertaining their growing circle of friends, and keeping the household in order.

As the years went by, Judy's greatest satisfactions were in seeing Rodney and Marcia grow up. Rodney often got into fights with other kids his own age, but he wasn't really a behavior problem. Marcia was a joy. As for the relationship between Judy and Ed, that was satisfying and comfortable for both.

On their tenth anniversary, Ed was able to present Judy with what she had always wanted, a small house in the suburbs. They moved out of their apartment in the outlying district of the city and into a pleasant, middle-class town about forty-five minutes commuting time from Ed's midtown office. Within a year, they felt as though they'd lived there forever.

When Marcia started eighth grade—Rodney was already in high-school—Judy started thinking seriously about her future. The kids didn't need to have her at home all day long any more. What should she do? She didn't want to sit around the house all day, or spend her time shopping, playing tennis, and getting her hair done.

Judy was now a thirty-eight-year-old woman. In the fourteen years of her married life, she had raised her children, run the household, and acted as a helpmate and companion to her husband. But, with the children getting ready to go out on their own, she felt she also had to find something to give her life new meaning and purpose. She was already a little bored with her life.

She discussed the problem with Ed, who, after a brief flare-up of male ego and insecurity, was reasonably sympathetic. They talked about hobbies, going back to school, and getting a job. But hobbies didn't really interest Judy much, and she felt she didn't have the patience for full-time schoolwork again. A job was obviously the best solution to the problem.

Judy, with Ed agreeing, felt that a job would not only get her back out into the world and give her a sense of direction, it would also enable them to put enough money away to send the kids to college, if everything worked out.

But what kind of a job? Judy had worked in retailing for almost three years, but that was a long time ago. Her experience might not be worth anything any more. Still, it was something to build on, and there were jobs available in the field. Judy decided to take a refresher course in purchasing at the local community college to give her a better shot at a good opening.

She scheduled her job-hunting to begin when Marcia entered high school, in about six months. Her course would be over then, too, which made the timing just about perfect.

One morning in September, Judy put on her most appropriate outfit, took the train into the city and started making the rounds of the department stores. She was excited, scared, and involved. And she felt at least a dozen years younger.

It was obvious from the first that Judy wouldn't have an easy time finding a job. The market was tight. Still, companies were on the lookout for good people. Every one of them treated her with interest and respect.

As she walked from store to store, Judy experienced what seemed a brand-new feeling. People were responding to her not as the mother of two children, not as a suburban housewife, but as a person with useful skills, a potentially valuable employee.

It took three trips into the city, and nine different interviews, to get a job offer. And the first one wasn't really right. It didn't pay much and it didn't give her much responsibility. But, on the third interview after that, Judy hit pay dirt.

One of the smaller junior department store chains needed an assistant buyer in women's sportswear. It was very much like the job Judy had left more than a dozen years ago. The pay wasn't fabulous, but it was good enough. And the company was talking about expanding its sportswear departments, which meant there were good advancement opportunities.

That night, Judy came home and told Ed she'd taken the job. She was to begin the next Monday. They celebrated over dinner that night, and Ed surprised Judy by presenting her with a beautiful brief case, "the women's executive model."

The first week on the job at Brandel's (we'll call it) was interesting and exciting. Judy toured the branch stores, getting to know the managers and junior buyers. She was shown the sort of merchandise she'd be helping to select. She settled into her office—a small, windowless cubicle below street level, but nonetheless hers. She soon personalized it with pictures and family photos.

During that week, she mastered the intricacies of the commuter train and the bus, she walked all the various routes she could take from the train terminal to her office, she sampled the various restaurants at lunch, she got to know her co-workers. She began to feel the first glimmerings of self-realization.

But the good feelings soon faded. She found that when she got home, at about six thirty, her family still expected her to prepare and serve dinner, though, to tell the truth, she was more exhausted than any of them.

There were troubles on the job, too. Her boss, also a woman, was five years younger than she was, and seemed to talk a million words a minute. Getting to know the manufacturers she had to deal with turned out to be a difficult task, and people didn't seem to have much patience when she made mistakes.

Even her pay check was a disappointment. Deductions for taxes and health insurance knocked a bigger chunk out of it than she'd expected. And after subtracting what she was spending on a commuter train ticket, lunches, and additional clothing for the job, she wasn't making very much at all.

Now she started to do some serious thinking. She was doing what she had been dreaming about for years: She was back on the job, at least semi-independent, using her own skills and knowledge. She had everything she had thought she wanted and it didn't look like much. What could she do now?

What she did was to apply herself to her job more fiercely than before, making a concerted effort to learn manufacturer's names, current styles, prices and discount schedules, what the competition was doing, etc. It was hard, demanding work.

But it paid off. She recommended that the chain buy a thousand pairs of discontinued ultrasuede pants. They were a bargain, but her boss was skeptical, though she gave her okay. The pants were featured in an ad and they sold out in three days. Then Judy pulled off a similar coup with some manufacturer's closeout sweaters.

And, suddenly, she was on top of the job. She knew it and so did everyone else. Her boss started asking her advice. Other buyers wanted to go out to lunch with her. She felt comfortable in what she was doing. She was contributing, on her own, and she knew it. She even got a raise.

For the next five or six months, things went beautifully. At home, the family pitched in with dinner, after only minimal grumbling, and everyone shared housekeeping duties.

On the job, Judy got the recognition she deserved. She settled in. But, as the months passed, she ran into another problem—boredom. She'd mastered her job. She could do her work with her eyes closed. She had the respect of her boss and her co-workers. But there wasn't any challenge to it any more.

Now she started to get a bit sloppy, but not so much that anyone else was likely to notice. She began to get depressed. And she started thinking about looking for a new job.

It was at this moment that Judy's boss came to her

with a proposal. She wanted to know if Judy would be willing to put together a new winter line from scratch. The store was going to upgrade its sportswear department.

Judy jumped at the idea. Before long, she was well into the new project, her zest for the job restored, her depression forgotten.

So far as I know, Judy is still working for Brandel's. She's a buyer now, not an assistant, and she's no longer handling women's sportswear, but women's better coats and suits. From what I understand, she's forever getting herself involved in new and satisfying projects.

Productive-Phase LIFE-CONTROL

The case history of Judy Savino is an interesting one because, as you'll see, she experienced two distinct productive phases simultaneously, on two different levels. And, in both, she used the identical LIFE-CONTROL principles to stay in charge of her life.

It's also interesting because her case is, in a sense, only peripherally involved with groups (the family and the work group). It is primarily the story of an individual who exercised personal leadership over her own affairs and over herself.

Judy Savino knew (without being taught, as it happened) how to handle the problems of the productive phase. But she might not have known; and if that had been the case, she could have either endangered her relationship with her family, or seriously injured her chances of keeping her job, or both.

Had she made some all-too-possible mistakes, she might have permanently damaged her chances for fulfillment. She could very easily have lost control of the main events in her life.

In the pages that follow, I intend to show you exactly what the productive phase is, from a process sense. I also intend to discuss the phase's unique problems and unique solutions. I'll discuss what Judy Savino did right and what she might have done wrong.

I chose Judy Savino's case history to illustrate the productive phase because it very neatly encompasses all the important elements, and because we all know people who are trying to work through process problems like hers.

But, I could just as easily have chosen:

- An industrial production line, after a new product has been introduced and debugged, where the main activity is to make as many units as possible, with maximum efficiency;
- An office situation, where the disruptions of resistance-testing are over, where the organization and format is well proven and the employees are doing their jobs;
- An army unit that has gone through the rigors of basic training and has taken up its ultimate assignment in the field;
- A classroom in which the novelty has worn off and the students are now getting down to business; or
- Any other group engaged in its chosen activity, and making genuine progress toward the goal to which it is committed.

As usual in LIFE-CONTROL, it's not the content that counts, but the process. And, also as usual, you can get the most out of the following analysis by substituting yourself and your situation for Judy Savino. If you do that, you'll find that the principles apply to your life quite as much as they did to hers.

Judy's Life Phases

Let's begin our dissection of the productive phase by first considering Judy Savino's life history, to see how she moved through her life cycle.

From the information I have, I'd say that she and Ed, like many young married couples, were clearly still in the resistance-testing phase of their lives in their first wedded years.

And, since both of them were still in the process of resolving their adolescent struggles for independence from their parents, they quickly moved into the resistance-testing phase of their marriage. It was during this period that they struggled to unify their lives and accept their new interdependent position.

That resistance-testing phase was complicated by the quick arrival of children. This especially intensified Judy's difficulties with the marriage, since she, unlike Ed, did not keep her job. That part of her life also changed. In her head, she was still involved in proving her independence to her parents. In her life situation, she'd suddenly become a mother and housewife.

If Judy had been able to stay at work for a year or two, if she and Ed had waited to have children, the two of them might have been able to make faster, smoother progress working through their personal and interpersonal problems.

As it was, the resistance-testing phase of their marriage was intense enough to cause Judy to separate from her husband briefly. But this separation apparently proved to them both how interdependent they'd become.

Judy's return signaled the end of her resistance-testing phase, both in terms of her marriage and in terms of her life. It was evidence that she had reached maturity.

(Incidentally, the only reason I can say this with some certainty is that I know what happened *after* she returned. Marital separations can take place and be ended without any change in phase, or followed by more separations and perhaps divorce.)

With the end of her resistance-testing phase, Judy went into the productive period of her life. (Evidently, Ed was already there, at least on the job. That would account for his steady promotions and raises.)

When Judy returned to Ed, her anxieties over the changes in her life wrought by marriage and children had resolved themselves. She felt a sense of stability and security.

Events, both internal and external, appeared to be in order.

Thus began a long period of productive life.

At this time, both parties to the marriage were engaged in working toward their core goals—helping each other (and the children) to grow emotionally, providing love, companionship, and protection for all, building the family's psychological and financial security.

Productivity and Boredom

During the productive phase, the lack of security and stability so disturbing to group members during resistance-testing is essentially gone. The group and its members have absorbed change. The new situation, marriage in this case, has become the norm rather than the old situation, the single life.

But something else may be gone, too, something valuable —excitement.

There's no question that the two most exciting phases of almost every cycle are the introductory phase and the resistance-testing phase. The introductory phase is full of the newness and promise that gives zest to life. The future seems bright and exciting. The resistance-testing phase offers the excitement of conflict and opposition, negative elements, to be sure, but stimulating.

Even the termination phase has its excitements—the sense of a job well done, the rewards of completion (often tangible), the disbanding of the group, the anticipation of a new introductory phase, and so on.

The productive phase, on the other hand, provides a much gentler, much more subtle brand of interest—the pleasures of moving toward a goal, the satisfaction of seeing the work get done, the gratification of following through on plans made during the introductory phase.

During this period, Ed derived his pleasure and excitement from advancing his career and from providing his family with its financial and material needs. There were enough changes in his job, as he moved up the ladder, to keep his interest up.

For Judy, the pleasures of the productive phase were largely vicarious, derived from her children's introductory phase of life. Marcia's and Rodney's growth and development provided her with all the feelings of excitement she needed.

But when her children's introductory phase began to end, Judy was potentially in trouble. If she hadn't realized that she needed to initiate a new subcycle, her life might soon have seemed empty and meaningless.

Many women find themselves in this situation in their middle years. When their children are almost grown up, they feel their life's work is done. They don't know how to find another way to be productive.

And, for that matter, men who have worked all of their lives at one profession often have the same feeling when they retire. They, too, have no idea how they can continue to be productive.

The same thing can be said for groups that have finished their jobs. They're at loose ends. They have no clear goals.

Judy followed good LIFE-CONTROL practice by seeking to solve her problem through a new subcycle, one that promised both excitement and involvement as well as substantial productive rewards with a minimum risk to her existing life structure. And, luckily, she was able to accomplish her aims. Not all women in this situation are so fortunate.

Interestingly, she repeated her previous behavior, her broad life-cycle actions, in this smaller, productive-phase subcycle. Here, too, she eventually reached a point where things were routine, where her job no longer excited her.

In that situation, many people are tempted to look for another job (though they may not be conscious of their actual motivation). This thought also crossed Judy's mind.

But her inclinations, and some fortunate circumstances, again saved her from that potentially disrupting course of action. Instead of moving on to another job, she found a new project where she was. She retained the value of her previous accomplishments and her hard-won status and built on them.

Of course, Judy might have been able to achieve the same effect by changing jobs. But the risks would have been greater. And, after a while, her history of job changing would have worked against her.

Four Miniature Phases in the Productive Phase

The productive phase, like the rest, can be thought of as having four separate smaller parts that, together, mirror the entire cycle of this period in Judy Savino's life.

For a different example of how the productive phase breaks down, let's consider Kissinger's 1975 efforts in the Middle East, as he got the two parties to agree to a partial Israeli pullback.

1. *The introductory part:* If you remember, before the disengagement pact was signed, there had been a breakdown in negotiations some six months earlier, the result of some strong resistance-testing by both parties.

During the hiatus between the breakdown and the resumption of negotiations, the American Government applied pressure on the Israeli Government, laying down some limits and doing its best to give the Israelis a sense of security, a difficult task under the circumstances but obviously not impossible.

At the same time, the United States provided the Egyptians with some reassurance, so that it, too, had enough of a sense of stability and security to be open to the renewal of negotiations.

Then, several weeks before Kissinger began the shuttle operation that produced an agreement, both sides felt secure enough to enter the productive phase of the project, to actually begin negotiating and working out the problems that existed between them.

Characteristically, it's at this time that the group members begin to regain some of the stability and self-confidence they lost when they first seriously confronted change, during resistance-testing. The anxieties begin to fade. They accept the new situation as the prevailing circumstance.

The productive phase, in a very real way, is the payoff of resistance-testing. The leadership has shown itself able to control events. It has responded to testing by providing group members with a sense of security and stability. As a result, the group and its members begin to believe they can do the job or accomplish their goals. It's in the introductory part of this phase that the group re-identifies its goals, strengthens its commitments, resolves its last remaining doubts and conflicts.

2. *The resistance-testing part:* If you'll recall, once negotiations between the Egyptians and the Israelis resumed, there were many optimistic statements for awhile. Then, suddenly, the Egyptians said they weren't going to renew the UN peace-keeping force's mandate, which was due to expire within the next few days. And the Israelis countered by saying they weren't going to negotiate an agreement with the Egyptians if they couldn't meet face-to-face (instead of having Kissinger act as a messenger).

This was the final bit of serious resistance-testing before the productive part of the productive phase. Both sides still felt a little insecure about what they were going to do, both needed to know that the leadership—the United States in this case—was still in the driver's seat. Neither side, as events proved, really was serious about its ploy. Egypt renewed the UN mandate after a moderate amount of pressure; Israel dropped its demand for face-to-face negotiations.

In most groups, especially those not dealing with war-or-peace issues, the resistance-testing part of the productive phase is notably different from the resistance-testing phase itself.

In that phase, the group's acting-up is of a decidedly negative and sometimes angry nature. The group's aim is to resist change and test the ability of the leader. But, in the productive phase, resistance-testing is essentially positive. At its best, it's good-humored and harmless, nothing more than a bit of overexuberance. At its worst, it consists of some *pro forma* grumbling and gripng, the kinds of noises that really signal all is well.

It's easy to understand why resistance-testing in the productive phase is so mild, when you think of the entire process. As I've said, resistance-testing is the inevitable result of change, since all change causes anxiety. Change generally threatens stability and security. It disrupts familiar patterns.

But, in the productive phase, the change amounts to a shift from uncertainty and insecurity to increased stability. To be sure, things are different. But they're different mainly in a positive way, so the resistance-testing is similarly positive.

It can turn sour, however. Any resistance-testing is a demand on leadership for guidance, for reassurance of control. If the leader doesn't pass the test, if he either ignores the group's misbehavior or overreacts to it, the group can rather quickly slip out of the productive phase and go back into full-scale resistance-testing.

Kissinger, if you'll recall, reacted to the situation quite wisely by expressing public misgivings about Egypt's threat not to renew the UN mandate. "Most unfortunate at this time," he said. And when Israel asked for direct negotiations, he reacted the same way—calmly, but taking a firm stand. If he'd accused either nation of attempting to sabotage the negotiations, he might have pushed the whole process back into resistance-testing.

3. *The productive part:* For the Egyptians and the Israelis, the productive part of the productive phase took place mainly during Kissinger's shuttle diplomacy. Each side worked with the practical problems presented, making compromises, adjustments, and modifications as necessary. Both nations were clearly interested in accomplishing their goal and were not about to let small differences stand in the way.

During this part of the phase, group members generally contribute generously of their talents and resources. By now, they have a major emotional commitment to the goal. They also feel reasonably comfortable and secure. They feel a part of the group.

In many groups, when this mood predominates, the group members start looking at themselves, at their performances and their contributions. They work to improve themselves and to grow. They make lasting friendships with others in the group. They become involved on a personal-thought-system level.

It's in this part of the phase—indeed, this part of the cycle—that group members are at their very best. They are committed and involved. They give to the best of their abilities. They so identify with the group and its goal that they would hardly know what to do with themselves if they suddenly left the group or if it disbanded for some reason.

For this reason, Prime Minister Rabin and President Sadat each found themselves defending the other's ideas to their own constituencies. In a sense, they became spokesmen for each other. Together (with Kissinger), they formed a stable group, devoted to a particular goal.

All of this is not to say that there aren't problems in this part of the phase. There are. First of all, there are practical problems, content problems. These never entirely disappear. Second, there may be problems with the members. If the phase goes on long enough, restlessness is bound to set in. There may be boredom.

But this is also the point at which the great accomplishments occur, as they most certainly did in the case of Egypt and Israel.

Unique Problems

At first thought, it might seem that the productive phase offers fewer opportunities for trouble than any other part of the cycle.

After all, it's in the productive phase that—

- A sense of stability and purpose reign, which has largely replaced the tension and anxiety of resistance-testing;
- The most difficult process issues, whether or not the group and its leadership can handle the content, have been decided positively;
- Group members have assimilated and internalized their new circumstance, and joined it to previous experiences; and
- Everyone is ready to work together to solve whatever practical problems may stand in the way of accomplishing the group's goal.

The productive phase is a time of work, action, and accomplishment. It is the most constructive period of the cycle. For the group, it's when there is the greatest movement toward the goal. For the member, it's when learning takes place, when skills are developed and mastered.

Yet, the productive phase, like the others, has its own unique problems, difficulties in process that can rear up and delay, dissipate, or even destroy the constructive accomplishments of the stage.

In order of their increasing severity, these problems are: first, a reversion, all the way back to the resistance-testing phase; second, inefficiency during productive-phase activities; and, third, untimely termination of the phase, or a productive phase that doesn't last as long as it should.

These problems are linked. Reversion, if it lasts for any length of time, can lead to inefficiency. Inefficiency, if it gets sufficiently intense, can bring about untimely termination of the phase.

But let's take them singly.

Reverting Back to Resistance-Testing

It wouldn't surprise me if the very name of this problem confuses you. How in the world, you might ask, can a group that's reached the productive phase, that's conquered its anxieties and accepted the new situation as the norm, go into reverse and wind up back in resistance-testing?

Oddly enough, this can be caused (at least in part) by the very confidence and trust a group usually feels toward its leader by the time it enters the productive phase.

After the initial honeymoon or introductory part of the phase, when the group is excited and pleased to be getting down to work at last, it shows its respect for its leader by doing a little resistance-testing. There's usually little doubt in the minds of the members that the leader can handle this easily.

This resistance-testing is not characterized by the negative storm and conflict of the resistance-testing phase. Instead, it has a positive note. It's good-humored. It usually consists of fooling around or goofing off.

And the leader usually reacts in kind, laughing with the group for awhile, then saying firmly (but without rancor), "Okay, let's knock it off now and get back to work." And the group immediately settles down and returns to the task.

Perhaps the most familiar example of this is the good class in school, in which almost every student is doing his work conscientiously and well, that every once in a while spends a half-hour of class time discussing trivia or making jokes. The teacher lets it go on until the students have "gotten it out of their systems" then steers the class back into productive work.

If the Leader Overreacts

Actually, this sort of thing happens in almost every productive group, be it a family, an industrial work crew, or a convention of clergymen. Usually, it amounts to no more than a brief interruption in production. But it can go haywire.

The trouble comes when the leader overreacts to the group's testing, when he takes it as a personal challenge or as a real threat to productivity, instead of seeing it as a sign of a loose, relaxed group, comfortable with him and with their work.

Such a leader may come down hard on the group or those members who are "making trouble," as he sees it. He may set up strict rules, work out punitive enforcement procedures and establish close supervision.

When a group in the productive phase is treated this way after some harmless resistance-testing, it's likely to turn angry and resentful. It will see the leader's reactions as a sign that he's not in control, after all. It will be sorely tempted to present him with some serious resistance-testing of the negative variety.

And, if the leader doesn't quickly come to his senses, he'll find that he and his group aren't in the productive phase any more, that they've reverted back to the resistance-testing phase.

I once saw this happen to an army training unit. It was in the third week of basic training and solidly in the productive phase; it was doing a good job learning various military skills, getting into good physical condition, adjusting to army life.

Then one afternoon, while a first lieutenant was leading the entire company in dismounted drill—"right face, left face, present arms, forward march," etc.—the young soldiers started to goof off, doing exactly the reverse of what the lieutenant ordered.

The lieutenant, feeling that his authority was being challenged, blew his stack. He collared the ringleaders and put them on KP (despite regulations against this punishment), and ordered that the unit be confined to barracks for the weekend.

In a single stroke, he pushed the young men all the way back into resistance-testing. The sick-call list promptly quadrupled, the barracks became sloppy (despite harsh cleanup efforts), and morale, once good, shriveled. The group remained sullen and rebellious throughout basic training.

And yet, the lieutenant could just as easily have had every

one of the men on his side. He could have greeted their fooling around with appreciative laughter, let them get it out of their systems, then said, "All right, let's see if you guys can do it right as perfectly as you càn do it wrong." And that, I have no doubt, would have been the end of that.

Even an alert and insightful member, an enlisted man in the unit, could have saved the situation if he'd told his unit, "Come on, let's show 'em what we can do when we want to," temporarily assuming leadership. But he'd have to do this before the appointed leader overreacted. Or, after his lieutenant overreacted, the enlisted man could have said, "Forget it, he's having a bad day."

The Dangers of Underreacting

Leadership can also trigger reversion by underreacting to the goofing-off typical of productive phase resistance-testing. If the lieutenant had said nothing, his unit would have misbehaved more and more seriously, until it got a reaction. By that time, punishment might have been the only way out.

Even in the productive phase, resistance-testing is the group's way of asking for guidance and reassurance. In essence, it wants to be told that everything is all right and that it should buckle down. When it doesn't get the guidance and reassurance it wants, the group is likely to ask again, more vigorously.

Something of this sort happened during a 1974 Cleveland-Texas baseball game, during "beer night," when management reduced the price of a glass of beer to ten cents. The crowd, whose original goal was to enjoy itself, soon found itself in the productive phase, having a blast.

But then the group started acting up. At first, it amounted to little more than boisterous cheering and heckling. The authorities—the stadium police, who had the leadership role in this situation—did nothing. Then the fistfights started to break out. Then bottle throwing, and finally, a very nearly full-scale riot.

What had happened was that the crowd had gotten frightened by its own power, numbers, and restless energy. It began to feel it was losing control and that scared it still further. Only when the police waded into the mob in force, swinging nightsticks, was control re-established and order restored. There were many arrests and minor injuries, a sad ending to the evening.

It needn't have happened. The team management could have prevented the riot in three ways:

First, it could have found some other way to draw a crowd than to provide vast quantities of inexpensive beer. It should have more carefully considered the potential consequences of this kind of promotion.

Second, once "beer night" was underway, management should have instructed the police to react quickly in event of trouble. That would have kept the disturbance to a minimum.

Third, management should have hired extra police and stationed them in highly visible locations. That alone probably would have given the crowd the sense of control and reassurance it needed.

I've illustrated what happens when a leader underreacts to productive-phase resistance-testing with a large group. But the same thing happens in small groups. They become unruly. They escalate their testing. I've seen it happen in classrooms.

In small or medium-sized groups, a wise member schooled in the principles of LIFE-CONTROL can temporarily (at least) take over the leadership when the leader doesn't act and give the "let's get back to work" signal. If the individual member is not isolated, or a scapegoat, or otherwise unpopular, this should get the group back on the beam.

If the Group Needs a Break

In some groups, productive-phase resistance-testing shows up not in fooling around, but in going off on a tangent, or diverging from the task at hand. A business meeting, for instance, may get away from the subject under discussion and begin debating the differences between indoor and outdoor tennis courts.

In that case, the leader should consider two major factors: (1) Whether or not he is pushing the group too hard and they need a break, increased socializing, in order to maintain efficiency; and (2) if he's providing the leadership the group needs. In this type of resistance-testing, too, the leader should neither overreact nor underreact.

By the way, tangents usually provide members with their best opportunity to take charge and direct the group back to its task. Group members may even have an advantage over leaders here, since they're more likely to know if their colleagues need a break, or when the socializing has gone on long enough.

The Many Factors Behind Inefficiency

Just because a group has reached the productive phase doesn't mean it will proceed, full-steam ahead, toward its goal. There are any number of factors that can intervene and cause members to give less than their best.

For example, when group members first enter the productive phase, when they've definitely passed resistance-testing, they may not be quite ready for full-scale production.

In this case, they may perform on a low plateau, slowly advancing toward the goal, at well below their best speed, apparently inert. Actually, this is a very active period. It is at this time that the group is internalizing what it has learned in the previous phases. It's as though they're gathering strength for a substantial leap forward.

That leap often occurs immediately after a minor bit of resistance-testing. If the leader passes, the group often shows a significant increase in performance. It's as if the group had waited for a green light, then took off.

I've often seen this while working with under-achieving students. After getting involved in special learning programs, going through distinct introductory phases and resistance-testing phases, they often spend three or four months on a no-progress plateau. Then, suddenly, they leap ahead.

What these children needed before they could benefit from their special training was time, time to absorb, assimilate, and test the information they had been given. When they finished that process, the change was dramatic.

So, leaders and group members should realize that time is an important factor in the productive phase. Groups may look inefficient at first, but they may merely be going through a period of assimilation prior to real production.

Furthermore, if the group is composed of several major subgroups, each with different skill levels, it won't make that leap forward until the most backward group is ready to move. The group members will try to advance together. Those in the vanguard will tend to wait for the stragglers.

The leader who thinks his "low plateau" group is inefficient is suffering from a misconception, from a misunderstanding of the process. Time will straighten him out, unless he gets impatient and overreacts in some way.

If the Skills Are Lacking

But groups can still move too slowly in the productive phase if some or all of the members of the group do not have the physical, emotional, or intellectual skills to do the job, at least with the proficiency required. This can happen no matter how much the members want to do what's asked of them.

There is something the leader can do about this situation. He can "program" those group members with the lowest skills, so that they can fully participate in the productive phase. He can allow the group members to develop the skills they need or help them, if need be.

I will give you an example.

A few years ago, a junior high school in a large urban

community called me in for a consultation after its first dance had ended in a riot. This was a school serving a large inner city population.

After interviewing representatives of the administration, faculty members, and students from each major group, I found that nearly everyone in the school had been in the productive phase, so far as the dance was concerned. And there had been very little trouble in the school prior to the dance.

From what I could discover, everyone had come to the dance with high hopes, excited about it, ready to have a good time. But the students began to act up. Eventually, they became quite disruptive. School officials had no choice but to shut down the dance prematurely, which caused even more trouble.

It soon became clear to me that the problem was a matter of skill levels. The students were acting up because they had never learned the social skills necessary to participate in an affair of this sort.

School officials wanted nothing more than to hold another dance, to clear the air. Was there anything I could recommend that would prevent trouble this time? I suggested that discussions about dances be held informally in the classrooms about the purpose of dances, how to behave and interact with others while there, how to act before, after, and during a dance, and so on.

The school followed my suggestions. Then it held another dance. This time, it was a delightful experience for all concerned. There was no disruption, no acting-up, no trouble worth the name. The skills of the group members had been appropriately reoriented to the situation.

There's no reason why a member can't perform this service for another member in his group. This should happen and often does when a highly skilled group member takes his lesser-skilled colleague aside and teaches him what he needs to know.

Part of the Team

Let's take the group a step further now. Let's say that the small, internal resistance-testing part of the phase is past, and that the members now have the skills they need in order to do the job.

At this point, most members of most groups have thoroughly committed themselves to the group goal. They're willing to give generously of their personal resources—mental, physical, and emotional—if that's what's required.

By this time, students will study far into the night and do extra reading, if necessary. Football players will "eat, sleep, and dream" their sport and give up all other pleasures, at least temporarily. Businessmen will take home brief cases full of work. Family members will display often astonishing self-sacrifice.

Group members feel this way because they now take a substantial part of their identity from their group. The experiences they've shared with other group members as they've gone through the travail of earlier phases have given them a profound sense of belonging. They've made a major emotional investment in the group.

This is especially true for individuals whose groups have worked through situations involving either great pleasure —the formation of a family, the birth of children, the successful struggle to accomplish a difficult task; or great pain—natural disasters, wars, illnesses and deaths, depressions or severe personal economic troubles, etc.

But it also applies to groups whose goals are of lesser importance, so long as they've successfully passed through the first two phases. Of course, the individual's emotional investment will be directly proportional to the group's meaning and importance to him.

In these situations, members feel part of the team, part of the family. Employees stop thinking of themselves as employees, but as part of the business. The groups are no longer "they," but "we." The member's aims and those of the group are now the same.

So it is for the volunteer political worker: If his or her candidate loses, it is a personal defeat. So it is for the production worker in a well-run factory: If the product doesn't sell, or if it turns out to be defective, or if the plant's good safety record is shattered by an accident, it is as much a personal disaster as a company setback.

Even when people play no direct role in a group, when they have only indirect or even imagined ties, they often take its failures or successes personally. You all know how you feel when your favorite pro sports team wins, or loses.

Wasting Momentum

And yet, a leader can dissipate this emotional commitment. He can turn a group that's ready to work into one that drags its heels, that loses valuable members with disturbing frequency, that fails despite its skills.

He can do this by acting improperly on the best of motivations, getting the job done as promptly and as well as possible.

In June, 1973, David Barker left Hogan Household Products, a large, New York-based manufacturer and marketer of soaps and cleansers, to join Fulsome & Newborne, its chief competitor, based in Chicago.

Barker had been assistant to the marketing director at Hogan, a staff position paying $28,000 a year. His main supervisory duties were administrative in nature. At F & N, he was made marketing director at $40,000 a year and put in charge of an eleven-man marketing team consisting of experts in advertising, displays, packaging, and related fields.

The first project asigned to the team after Barker arrived was to introduce a new household cleanser and make it an instant competitor to Ajax and Comet. Barker was promised a bonus if he succeeded. But he hardly needed the incentive.

He was determined to gain a reputation as a go-getter. Unfortunately, this exemplary attitude eventually caused his downfall.

The marketing team, which had handled several projects of this kind and was a close-knit, highly sophisticated team, passed through the introductory phase and the resistance-testing phase with hardly a ripple. It was accustomed to handling this sort of change.

Barker began well enough. An outwardly genial and friendly man, and apparently a great improvement over his perpetually angry predecessor, he had members of his team hoping for the best.

But his newness to the job soon betrayed him. His emotional investment didn't equal that of the team members; it couldn't, since he hadn't shared their previous experiences on the job.

Because he didn't know where the group was coming from and because he was so eager to prove himself, David Barker then proceeded to make a string of errors.

First, he decided to oversee every detail of the new promotion personally. He wanted everything to go perfectly. He watched over the point-of-purchase man as he worked out a supermarket display. He sat in while the media man selected advertising space, making frequent "suggestions." He personally reviewed the packaging designs, choosing one the product-design team member didn't care for.

In essence, he oversupervised. There are few things a leader can to do a group that are as inhibiting and disturbing as oversupervision. It implies lack of trust. This damages the group members' self-confidence and their sense of group identity. It reduces member commitments, and, eventually, efficiency.

I'm not suggesting that he should have abandoned his group to its own whims. He should have kept an eye on things (especially at the beginning of the project), stimulated ideas, answered questions (or obtained answers from technical experts), stepped in when asked or when serious problems cropped up.

But he shouldn't have gotten involved on a moment-to-moment basis. He should have let the group exercise the responsibility it had developed. He should have seen himself mainly as a consultant, particularly after the work got going.

Second, Barker set some strict limits. Since this was a major project, he said, there would be no days off until it was completed. Lunch hours were to be just that—an hour, no longer. Coffee breaks were limited to two a day. And he said he hoped no one would take a sick day unless he were really ill.

But the group didn't need limits. If anything, it was more committed to the project than Barker was. He didn't know it, but many a team member had worked evenings and weekends on major projects like this in the past, and without urging. So Barker's petty rules made the members angry and resentful.

Third, Barker set out to establish a "strictly business" atmosphere. He openly frowned on any digressions from the subject at hand. He discouraged what he called "time-wasting" discussion. He made it clear to members who had opinions of their own that they should keep them to themselves. He tried to keep socializing to a minimum.

What Barker didn't realize—and his inexperience was probably to blame here—was that the productive phase is the time to give members their head, to create a relaxed atmosphere, to encourage discussion, to bring differences of opinion out into the open.

Fourth, Baker was incredibly alert to his team's errors and mistakes, but he was deaf, dumb, and blind when it came to work that was handled particularly well or simply done properly.

For instance, he instantly realized that his media man had forgotten *Redbook* when drawing up the initial ad campaign. But he made no comment when the same man got a terrific package deal from CBS on daytime game-show spots.

And he immediately noticed a misprint on the "cents-off" coupon. But he had nothing to say when the member responsible managed to get a four-color printing job for the price of a three-color job by cleverly blending shades.

Improper Reinforcement

In these cases, Barker was making two mistakes simultaneously:

First, he was reinforcing bad behavior. I've seen this happen between parents and children more times than I care to remember. The first- or second-grade child brings home 95s on his report card, only to find his parent concentrating on the 5 percent that's wrong and ignoring the main accomplishment.

By the time the child is in the third or fourth grades, he's getting the first half of his tests right but not completing the second half. He's been conditioned to act this way because he gets the greatest payoff and reward from his parents, the most attention, for what he does wrong, not what he does right.

Second, he was not reinforcing productive behavior. Just about the best thing a leader can do to ensure efficiency in the productive phase is to reinforce the group members when they do their work well, to let them know he approves of and appreciates their efforts.

This encourages the members to do more of the same, since rewards of this sort are, in part, what productive activity is all about in the first place. It also deepens their sense of group identity and their commitment to the job.

One excellent way the leader can do this is to help each member see himself as part of the whole, by putting his contribution into perspective and showing him how important his efforts are and what roles others play. If he's given a perspective, he'll not only have increased feelings of self-worth, he'll also have greater respect for the contributions of his colleagues.

Another good way to reward a member for valuable work is to provide him with opportunities for growth. Barker, for instance, might have given his media man an assistant, or a raise, or a promotion to a more responsible job.

The third way to reward is to do it literally—give raises, give public praise, give recognition, etc. This benefits the member, of course, but it also benefits the group, since it reinforces the member's productive behavior, and not only for the rewarded member but for others in the group who need an example.

Tension Relief

One manager I knew in a position similar to Barker's made a different sort of error. He frequently used members of his team to relieve his own tensions. He shouted at them, he snubbed them, he made snide remarks, he disparaged their skills, and so on. In most cases, his subordinates had transgressed in some small ways, but he magnified each transgression, then pounced on it.

I'm sure you can imagine what this did to his team. As a result of his outbursts, the team members became secretive and fearful. They withdrew, taking as few risks as possible, for fear of making errors and getting blasted for their trouble. They tended to protect one another. The manager became not their leader, but their common enemy.

This "tension relief" syndrome is very common in families. I've done it myself. The most recent occasion took place after an extraordinarily busy and tense forty-eight-hour period, in which the days were filled with consultations and the evenings with emergencies at the clinic.

I arrived home at seven thirty at the end of the second day grumpy, tired, and irritable. My three children, who'd been playing well together, started fighting. I told them to stop it. They didn't. I told them more sharply. No response. I shouted.

Well, that got a response. They stopped. And as for me, I felt wonderful. All the tension that had been building up was suddenly released. I'd done something I needed to do. It was better than a martini.

Fifteen minutes later, the kids were playing together again as if nothing had happened. It was almost as if they knew and accepted the temporary role they'd played, lightning rod for my tensions.

All parents use their children—and each other—as tension relievers occasionally. So do all bosses. Practically every leader of every group does it from time to time. And it's not damaging. It may even be helpful, if those affected can discuss what happened and why afterward.

But when the leader constantly uses the group members for tension relief, or when the person picks on one individual time and time again, the tension reliever syndrome is very destructive. It requires that the group member (or members) perform the superhuman task of relieving the leader's very considerable tensions while handling his own at the same time.

The last time I heard about David Barker, he'd left F & N, under somewhat ambiguous circumstances, and gone back to New York to a lesser job in a pharmaceutical house. As for the new cleanser, it never made it to the national marketplace. It was test-marketed in a few areas, then dropped.

Did it have to happen? Could Barker have succeeded? Frankly, I don't know. I'm no expert on the content problems he and his group had to solve. But I do know he could have handled the process issues more intelligently.

Could a group member have altered the outcome? Again, I can't talk about content. But an insightful group member might have helped maximize production within the group.

The team's senior member, for example, might have taken some time to give Barker the frame of reference he so badly needed; he might have explained how the team had functioned in the past, what it had accomplished, what it preferred, how it worked best, etc.

If these comments had been presented in the clear interest

of improved productivity, Barker might have been very receptive to them. At the very least, he would have listened. In this way, a member or members might have given their leader the guidance he needed, thus assuming the leadership role in a very real way.

The members might also have set up their own reward system by establishing a series of goals—a schedule perhaps, or a flow chart. Then they might have rewarded themselves as they reached each plateau, perhaps with an off-hours party.

Certainly, a senior member of the team could have taken over the reinforcer role, at least in part, whether or not Barker was aware of it. He could have given recognition where it was due and correction where it was needed. This might have kept the group headed toward its goal, despite Barker.

Task-Oriented Versus Relationship-Oriented Leaders

David Barker was a classic example, inept though he was, of a task-oriented leader. That is, he was concerned primarily with getting the job done. He didn't really give a darn about how the rest of the group regarded him.

But there is another kind of leader, the relationship-oriented leader. This kind of person is concerned mainly with his relationship to the group members and the members' relationship to each other.

Relationship-oriented leaders are extremely sensitive to group members' needs, feelings, and opinions. But that doesn't mean that they, too, can't turn a productive-phase group, one that's rarin' to go, into an inefficient, disorganized mob.

I came across just such a man while doing some consulting work for a large conglomerate. He—I'll call him Sam Baltzell—was plant manager of a good-sized refrigerator-manufacturing facility in a big midwestern city.

Baltzell had been plant manager for nearly seventeen years before our paths crossed. During that time, he'd acquired an enviable reputation for fairness and honesty. It was said that, large as his plant was, it functioned like one happy family.

One of the conglomerate's vice presidents, who briefed me on the situation, said that the refrigerator plant was— or at least it had been—unique in the company. There was an enormous amount of socializing between employees, both on the job and off, and between employees and management.

He showed me the plant house organ—one of the most elaborate of its kind I've ever seen—which listed company parties, bowling leagues, boat trips, picnics, and similar events.

It also dealt with such personal items as births, deaths, marriages, promotions, retirements, and new employees. These items were inextricably intermingled with business items, such as production goals, safety records, quarterly sales figures, car-pool pickup points, and new equipment ordered or installed.

And each issue carried a personal message from Baltzell, and I do mean personal. His words were warm, friendly, sympathetic, and open. Thus he shared some of his problems and doubts with his employees. They were messages of a man who wanted very much to be liked, and it was very difficult not to oblige him.

Before we discussed the plant's current troubles, I asked the conglomerate's vice president about its past record. The plant was never very efficient, he told me. Sam never wanted to fire anyone, even incompetents. His bonuses were often too large and given on the basis of need, not merit. The work force was too large.

But the "old man" had known Sam from the early days and had sentimental feelings toward him. He'd been disturbed by the plant's efficiency record, but he'd never done anything more than send Sam a chiding letter.

Then I asked the executive to describe the current situation. He told me that the refrigerator division, despite the inefficiencies in Sam's plant, had been in the black for years (though he hinted it could have made much more money). For the last three years, however, it had been in the red. The "old man" was now under extreme pressure from the board of directors to close it down.

It wasn't that the refrigerator market had gone sour. In fact, sales were actually up. But plant expenses were up even more, to a degree that couldn't entirely be accounted for by wage and material-cost increases.

"It's inefficiency," the vice president told me. "Sam's plant is the least productive one in our system, on a man-hour basis. And I'd say we have about six months to correct the problem."

And so I was sent to the plant to see what I could do. Baltzell turned out to be as described, a friendly man in his late fifties who seemed to know every employee by his first name (and vice versa). He gave me free reign in the plant, kept me occupied socially in the evenings, and treated me like a good friend. But that was the way he treated everyone.

What I found was that Baltzell's plant was suffering from a bad case of oversocializing. He'd set out to create a family atmosphere and wound up creating something like a real family, complete with nepotism, favoritism, indulgence of nonproductive members, overly democratic decision-making, toleration of adolescent acting-up, etc.

Baltzell's management group liked him, to a man. But they didn't respect him. They saw him as a colleague, a buddy—not a leader. And they treated him appropriately. I sat in on one meeting where he was cut short, contradicted, and voted down without recourse.

If anything, Sam had too much empathy. He could always see the other fellow's side, even to his disadvantage (and the firm's). He didn't know how to be cruel, or even firm. He was, in short, a pushover.

Over the years, Sam had done his best to remove the barriers between labor and management. He'd struggled to get himself accepted as one of the boys. And he'd succeeded. It looked like a triumph, but it was really a disaster.

Unknowingly, Sam had violated one of LIFE-CONTROL's cardinal principles: He'd made himself into a group member, leaving his group—his plant—with no leader or boss. Even the plant's management group had no place to go when it needed reassurance that someone was in charge, when it needed guidance and direction.

The management group tried to fill the gap itself, by taking over the direction of plant operations as best it could. But it wasn't equipped for the job. It had neither the internal unity nor the skill.

In the end, the corporation kicked Sam upstairs. He was made director of employee relations for the entire conglomerate, a job perfectly suited to his talents. The most promising member of the plant's management group was made plant manager. The others were transferred, individually, to other operations.

And the plant is still making refrigerators.

Sam lost sight of the firm's primary goal, to produce and make a profit. Instead, he almost exclusively emphasized its secondary goal, to give employment and to help employees live a secure and satisfying life.

Though these examples illustrate the LIFE-CONTROL principles I've been talking about here, they may seem to be special cases. Not so. The content in your group may differ from the content in my examples, but the process will be the same.

If, during its productive phase, your group is conducted without sufficient regard for its members' needs, efficiency will drop, whether the cause is overly dominant leadership or overly retiring leadership. Unless someone, member or leader, takes corrective action, there will be trouble.

There is yet another reason for group inefficiency in the productive phase, restlessness. But I'll treat that in the next section, since it can have more serious consequences than simple inefficiency.

A Foreshortened Productive Phase: Restlessness

The productive phase, as I've said, does not offer either the excitement of anticipation characteristic of the introductory phase or the excitement of conflict inherent in resistance-testing. Its joys are more subtle ones—a feeling of accomplishment, the rewards of seeing the job get done, a sense that all is well, an atmosphere of comfort and security.

If the productive phase is relatively brief, if the job is wrapped up quickly and a new cycle begun, and if the leader leads according to the members' needs, this part of the cycle is likely to be a positive experience for most or all of the group.

But, in many cases, productive phases have no natural termination point. The productive phase of life may continue until death finally ends it. A job may go on and on and on, for decades. A relationship may continue in the productive phase (once it's gone through the two earlier phases) for as long as the participants survive.

In cases like these, group members eventually get restless. They sooner or later feel the need for some kind of excitement, something to rekindle the spark, something to give them a renewed sense of interest in the job, a renewed feeling of vitality.

There are two main reasons for this restlessness. The most obvious is the routine into which most tasks eventually fall. And, when a task becomes routine, it fails to engage the hearts and minds of those who work at it. Boredom replaces satisfaction.

The second cause is the opportunity the productive phase provides for self-examination. Individuals aren't really able to look at themselves during the introductory phase or during resistance-testing. They don't have a sufficient sense of security.

But the productive phase brings with it that security. And this allows group members to examine their performance, to consider themselves as individuals, to reflect on their relationships with others in the group, to start to work out their personal problems. A lot of autoanalysis takes place at this time.

The result, quite often, is a feeling of restlessness about the present situation. Group members frequently feel that the productive phase tasks in which they're engaged are inhibiting their growth and development.

Incidentally, leaders are just as subject to these feelings as members are. They, too, get restless, feel vaguely dissatisfied, wonder if their job is really the most certain path to self-fulfillment.

I could cite example after example here, but I'm sure you know from personal experience what I'm talking about. I'm talking about the urge to change jobs, to move, to cheat on your spouse, to switch friends, to alter habits, to shake up your routines—for no good reason except restlessness.

So far as the group is concerned, this urge, if its members or its leader act upon it, can cause inefficiency, minimize the accomplishments of the productive phase, bring the phase to a premature end, or even destroy the group's viability. Members or leaders affected by restlessness often give less than their best. Sometimes, they drop out entirely.

So far as the member is concerned, restlessness can be an extremely self-destructive emotion. Restlessness can disrupt steady progress toward meaningful goals, destroy relationships that have taken years to build, even damage a person's identity, by partially or completely separating him from the group or groups from which he derives it.

Solving the Problem

Restlessness, then, is a problem that begs for a solution. Fortunately, there are several that are consistent with the principles of LIFE-CONTROL, solutions that do not depend on specific content, but that can be applied in a process way:

1. *Leader enthusiasm:* If restlessness is not a major prob-

lem—at least not yet—a leader who communicates his ardor and zeal may be able to keep it from getting out of hand. This technique is often used in sports. It's why pep talks and "holler guys" often succeed in inciting their teams to greater effort.

But leader enthusiasm has its limitations. It isn't much good against serious restlessness, unless it's combined with other actions. And it loses its effect after awhile, even against minor restlessness.

But the fact that it's only temporary is no reason to dismiss it. The very nature of the restlessness problem makes permanent solutions unlikely.

2. *The Hawthorne effect:* Years ago, mental health professionals studied the Western Electric assembly plant in Hawthorne, Illinois, to find out what factors decreased or increased worker efficiency, among other things.

What they discovered was that *any* outside attention stimulated productivity—filling out questionnaires, an observer on the scene, a check of production rates, tourists watching the operation, anything at all.

Evidently, outside attention makes a group member more interested in what he is doing, perhaps because others are interested in it. How much of an effect this has, of course, depends on the source, intensity, and length of the outside attention.

If the foreman's five-year-old son stops by for a few minutes "to see how the big machines work," the effect will be brief and minimal. But if a member's nubile twenty-one-year-old daughter does exactly the same thing, the short-term benefits may be remarkable.

The Hawthorne effect is related to what I call—

3. *The novelty effect:* Studies have shown that even minor changes in a group's routine or environment can have a salutary effect on productivity. By minor, I mean something as trivial as changing seating arrangements in a classroom, or painting the inside of an office, or installing a coffee machine.

Such changes alter a group member's perceptions of the

task and his role in it. They may cause a little resistance-testing and some increased socializing, both of which, in the end, would reinforce group identity in a favorable way.

I know of an organization that used to distribute pay checks through the interoffice mail. This method worked well enough, but the company treasurer came up with an improvement, a change she thought would lend a personal touch.

One Friday, instead of giving the checks to the mail room, she sorted them, floor by floor, office by office, and took them around herself. She personally handed the proper check to each individual employee.

This insignificant change caused a mild sensation. Employees talked about it, joked about it, began to anticipate it with pleasure. It eventually became a tradition. And the chief bookkeeper became known as the "money lady," a title she bore with good humor.

What she'd done was to add a personal payoff to the monetary one each employee received. It was as if the treasurer was complimenting the employee on a job well done. In a small but important way, every employee had been given a kind of raise, some personal attention.

Many industries rely on the novelty effect to capture their customers' interest, especially the auto industry. Every year it brings out new models. These cars aren't really too different from last year's, but they're enough to draw attention.

As a result potential buyers, tired of the old models, are given a new, face-saving reason to look again, perhaps to buy.

I've often heard this yearly model change decried as a waste of money. Maybe so. But it's really a two-way street. The industry uses it to attract buyers. The public uses it to help break the monotony of everyday life. Everyone benefits.

Unfortunately, the auto industry is better at using the novelty effect outside of itself than it is internally, on the assembly line. Boredom and restlessness among auto workers is one of the industry's knottiest problems. Perhaps auto makers should come out with internal "model changes" at least once a year.

4. *A change of scene:* One usually effective way to rouse a group from its doldrums is to make major changes in its environment, of either a temporary or a permanent nature.

In a business office, for instance, the occupants of individual cubicles might be shifted around. Or, work hours might be staggered a bit, so that some people arrive fifteen minutes earlier and leave fifteen minutes earlier.

In a family, changing the environment might amount to going on a weekend trip or even a vacation.

In school, the effect might be accomplished by means of a field trip, or holding a class outdoors under a tree.

Sooner or later, of course, the group will become accustomed to the new environment. It may get restless again. Then you'll have to think of something else.

5. *A new project:* An excellent way to spark the interest of a group that's productive but restless is to initiate a new project. Very often, what you need will appear naturally, as the initial goal is accomplished.

A construction crew, for instance, will no sooner finish off one building than it's assigned to a new one, with new problems and new challenges. A student, as soon as he finishes one course (or one semester or one year), will move naturally into a new one. A mother may hardly finish cleaning up the lunch dishes before the little ones come home, asking her to play with them.

Some groups or individuals, however, continually deal with change. Advertising agencies are always at work on a new campaign, sometimes many at the same time. Taxi drivers let off one fare, then pick up another. In these and similar cases, change may become part of the routine. It may no longer excite and interest.

What's needed here is more significant change, unexpected change, major new projects that require major new efforts from both group and member.

6. *Growth, development, and learning:* So far, I've been largely talking about external change, attempts to rouse restless members from the outside. If the problem is really serious, however, members may be reachable only from the inside.

If you're a group leader, the most effective action you can take to keep group members involved and interested in the job is to help them grow and develop, or at least provide them with learning activities.

Not long ago, I saw this point beautifully illustrated in a most unlikely setting, a child's birthday party. The child, a ten-year-old boy, had invited about a dozen of his friends, mostly schoolmates, to celebrate the occasion. To keep them entertained and occupied until cake and ice cream were served, his parents had hired a magician, an older man who happened to be a retired policeman.

For about twenty minutes, the magician went through his routines faultlessly. He even had a little line of patter that kept the kids laughing. Then the mother started setting the table in the dining room, which was visible from the living room, where the magician was performing.

Even a clever magician is no competition for visions of ice cream and cake. All the youngsters started fidgeting in their seats and looking toward the dining room. It took the magician a few minutes to figure out what was happening. But, once he knew, he solved the restlessness problem in a jiffy.

He did a particularly complicated sleight-of-hand trick with some coins, then smiled innocently and asked, "Is there anyone here who might be interested in learning how to do that? I've always wanted to teach it to someone."

Cake and ice cream had to wait that day, until the magician had given every boy at the party a lesson on sleight-of-hand.

This may sound like a trivial example, but I've seen exactly the same thing done in the classroom, in an industrial setting, in a family, in social groups, in just about every setting. The content was different in each case, but the process was the same.

A Chance for Self-Improvement

Basically, it involved the leader giving the group member a chance to improve himself, to learn, to take on more responsibility, to advance within the organization, to master a new and valuable skill, to undertake more important duties, etc.

Over a period of time, one or all of these techniques can be used to combat restlessness, in any combination. The only caution to remember, when introducing anything new into a stable situation, is that if the change is really significant the group will begin a new cycle, complete with introductory phase, resistance-testing phase, and so on. If you want to avoid that, keep the changes as small as possible.

So far, I've been talking about the things a leader can do to help a restless group member or members. But there's no reason a leader can't take any one of these actions on his own behalf, when he finds himself getting restless.

For that matter, there's no reason a member can't help himself by introducing some novelty into the scene, changing his environment, volunteering for a new project, or finding ways to grow and develop within the group context.

In many situations, an individual member might be able to help others in the group if and when they start suffering from the restlessness syndrome. He can share some of his enthusiasm, or give a pep talk, or throw a new project toward the restless member, or even teach him something new.

Group members and leaders can also deal with their own personal feelings of restlessness in other ways—in their private lives, during the time they spend away from the group. There are all sorts of options open to group members here, activities that will bring new excitement and vitality to their lives without adversely affecting their position in the group or its activities.

The group member or leader can take on a new hobby, he can get involved in a totally new off-hours activity, he can make new friends, he can moonlight, he can go back to school, he can enter a contest, he can make plans for the future, he can take up a new sport, he can do just about anything new and exciting.

If what he does has no relation to the group that bores him, the new activity won't help him there, at least not directly. But it may allow him to tolerate the routines and patterns that have become monotonous to him in his main group—his job, for example.

And, in time, that on-the-job boredom may cure itself. As a group member or leader grows in terms of sophistication and maturity, he'll probably find that his interest can be sparked by small, subtle changes in his work or in the group. He'll have a different perspective about his activities. He'll see things he wasn't able to see at an earlier stage in his development.

Take, for instance, a violinist in a symphony orchestra. He may start to get bored after he's mastered the repertoire and performed it a dozen times. But he may also be able to hear, and enjoy spotting, subtle differences from performance to performance.

He may take to comparing acoustics in one concert hall and then another. He may notice when the conductor is "on" and when he isn't. He may get pleasure from detecting differences between audiences, etc., etc.

The deeper your appreciation and understanding of the events that make up your life, the more satisfaction and excitement you'll get from them, even if it's not the thrill of something totally new, but a quieter, more modest kind of pleasure.

I've watched this happen in my own life.

The experience I had working with racially troubled schools and communities in the late 1960s was more intensely interesting and exciting than anything I'd ever done before. Everything and everyone was in resistance-testing. I know I'll never have that sort of experience again.

But I'm getting a different kind of excitement from my work now. I get a vicarious thrill when I watch a new therapist come onto the staff of my institute and begin to develop. I share in the excitement when I watch my men tackle a new project, or when one of my therapists tells me how one of his most troubled patients is starting to make solid progress.

For me, there is always a newness to life, an excitement that's there if you're willing to see it. The productive phase has been far and away the best part of my life and I hope it lasts as long as I do.

What I'm saying, I suppose, is that the final answer to the restlessness we all feel from time to time during the productive phase is to avail ourselves of the excitements life always offers us.

General Problems

Once a group has reached the productive phase, it has attained a high degree of stability and security. Most of the process problems it confronted in the two earlier phases, problems with underlying group function, have been solved or worked through.

For this reason, the general difficulties most groups face at this time are largely practical. They mainly involve content, not process. In a way, they boil down to a single question, How can we get the job done most efficiently, or with the greatest satisfaction for all?

Still, there are some process difficulties that can crop up. Some process problems may still be unresolved by this time, or new ones may appear as a result of the group's new circumstances.

As always, these fall into three major categories:

• Problems of leadership in which the group members are faced with either an absent leader or one who mis-

handles problems, or one who is out of phase with the group;
- Problems of membership in which the group must deal with an antisocial individual or members who are out of phase; and/or
- Problems of circumstance, external events that affect the group in some unexpected way.

These are the problems I intend to deal with in this section.

But, before I do, let me remind you once more that in the pages that follow, as well as those that have gone before, the problems and their solutions apply to your group as well as they do to the case histories and examples I cite here.

And that holds no matter what groups you belong to, large or small, closely knit or far-flung. It also holds whether you consider yourself a leader or a member, for, as you've seen, those positions are often interchangeable. And it holds whether you are a man or a woman.

But on to specifics. . . .

Problems of Leadership

Usually, by the time a group reaches the productive phase its members, individually and collectively, are ready to assume responsibility for getting the job done.

In a sense, the leader has completed the most difficult part of his job. He's stimulated ideas during the introductory phase and helped the group come to a commitment. He's provided the necessary guidance and direction during resistance-testing. He's given the group the sense of stability it needs in order to proceed.

But the leader's job is not quite over. He must see to it that the work takes place as planned. He must make sure that no loose ends are left hanging. The final responsibility is always his. That's what makes him a leader.

I covered most of the productive-phase leadership problems in the previous section. But a few remain, difficulties or circumstances that don't directly relate to any phase. The first of these is:

Absence or withdrawal. In previous phases, the leader's constant presence was vital; in this, it is not. Group members no longer need constant supervision. They not only know what has to be done, they're usually ready and willing to do it.

For this reason, leader presence isn't vital during the productive phase. This is the time the leader can close his office door and catch up on his personal work, or when he can get in an occasional golf game, or take off in the middle of the week to spend some time with his family, or take that long-delayed vacation.

This is the time the leader can most successfully delegate authority to his right-hand man, giving him the job of overseeing the work, making sure everything goes as it should, and working out solutions to common, practical production problems.

But the leader should never completely withdraw from the group, unless, of course, he's stepping aside for a new leader. Even in the productive phase, when members are working well on their own, he has a numbers of functions to perform:

First, he must be available to help solve major problems, either of the content or nuts-and-bolts variety, or of the process variety—increased acting-up, inefficiency, restlessness, and the like.

Second, he must be around to reinforce work well done, to help give members a sense of group identity and involvement, thereby insuring the continuation of the productive phase.

Third, he must be available, at least occasionally, for no particular purpose other than to "show the flag," to maintain the members' sense of security by reassuring them that someone is in charge of the store.

I know of a Broadway director who labored mightily to bring a musical to the stage, going through a very difficult resistance-testing period both internally and externally.

Initial out-of-town reviews were dreadful and there was a major cast rebellion. But he held on and brought in a hit.

Then he promptly vanished for six months, to a Caribbean island hideaway without a telephone or a mailbox. When the producer finally found him and brought him back, that cast rebellion was in full flower again and the show was in serious trouble.

I'm not saying he shouldn't have taken that Caribbean vacation, but a month or so should have been sufficient. Even after that, there was no need for him to take over the day-to-day direction of the production. All he had to do to prevent serious trouble was to act as a consultant, stopping in once every week or ten days, making himself reasonably available if something went wrong.

Mishandling problems. With a group in the productive phase, the leader can usually count on a lot of help in dealing with all sorts of problems. But that hardly means things can't go wrong.

We've already seen in the section on unique problems in the productive phase how a leader can mishandle process difficulties. In addition, he can—and probably will—make mistakes with content problems.

If he's a factory owner, for instance, he might among other things order too much of a raw material, set prices too high or too low, require too much output from antiquated machinery.

If he's a teacher, he might forget to give an assignment, or make a mistake grading papers, or answer a factual question incorrectly, and so on.

If he's a parent, he might mishandle family finances, smash up the car, forget to have the new house inspected for termites, etc.

Problems such as these are bound to occur, so long as people remain imperfect. But there is one LIFE-CONTROL rule that may give general aid, a directive that applies as much to content as it does to process: Anticipate problems.

If you're going to be a really effective leader, you'll have to do your best to look ahead, to spot difficulties before they happen, to figure out how to avoid them if you can, or prepare to deal with them if they're inevitable.

The leader who gets so caught up with the present that he doesn't give any thought to the future is making a serious error, in my judgment. What's more, he's making a correctable error. All he has to do is remember what his responsibilities are.

Incidentally, this area provides members with an excellent opportunity to exercise leadership. There's nothing that says members can't anticipate problems and prepare for them. If they do, they'll not only be helping their groups, but also advancing themselves in the hierarchy and making opportunities for themselves to take on further leadership responsibilities.

Out-of-phase leaders. If, in its productive phase, a group finds itself with a leader who knows his role, who is sensitive to members' needs, who knows when and how to exert authority, and above all, who knows how to get the job done, it can hardly ask for more.

Leaders like this abound. They're especially visible in the sports world. You know them because their teams win year after year. I'm talking about the Vince Lombardis, Paul Browns, Red Auerbachs, Johnny Woodens, and Charles Finleys of this world.

You'll note that this list doesn't include any prototypical "nice guys." Well, you'll remember that I said personality wasn't a decisive factor in leadership. If a leader inspires confidence in his ability, if he's comfortable with his own style, and if he's sincerely interested in his job and the welfare of the group members, he doesn't have to be humble and self-effacing.

A productive-phase group will also have no complaints if it find itself with a leader who's flexible enough to adapt to any phase. Men and women who can do this effectively aren't very common but they do exist. I've often seen them in families, successfully leading their groups through the euphoria of the introductory phase, the conflicts of resistance-testing, and the quiet satisfaction of the productive phase.

When a group doesn't find itself with any one of these leader types, it often goes out and gets someone who fills the bill. Or, the out-of-phase leader self-selects himself out of the picture and hands over the power to the person who's right for the job. The initiative for change can come from either direction.

But there are times when a group finds itself with a leader who isn't right for its phase. For example, a productive-phase group might come to the realization that its leader is basically an introductory-phase type, someone whose main interest is ideas, not production.

I can easily imagine a classroom full of adults bent on learning the essentials of television repair, say, so they can go out and earn a living, only to be frustrated by a teacher who's an expert in the field but would much rather spend classroom time talking about laser beams and holograms than transistor replacement.

Or, a productive-phase group might discover that its leader is firmly embedded in his own little resistance-testing phase and is acting as though the rest of the world is in there with him, constantly setting up rules and inventing punishments for transgressors.

There's a name for a man like this: martinet. He demands that his group strictly adhere to the rules, whether they fit the situation or not. The military services are full of such men and industry isn't far behind.

Or, a productive-phase group might come to understand that its leader is a termination-phase person, someone who enjoys looking backward, keeping records and scrapbooks, making everything as tidy as possible.

This is often the case when Grandpa or Grandma heads up the family. The rest of the members may be well into the productive phase, working efficiently toward family goals. But, if they're not doing things the traditional way, Grandma or Grandpa will be upset. Newfangled ways of doing things, however effective, will upset their sense of order.

A well-motivated, closely knit group in its productive phase may be able to progress toward its goal under any one of these leaders, since much of the leadership drive by this time rests with the group rather than with the individual nominally in charge.

If it knows where it's going and it knows how to get there, a productive-phase group may be able to swallow the digressions of an introductory phase-type leader, the restrictions of a resistance-testing-type, or the backward thinking of a termination phase-type and keep going in its preferred direction.

But that depends on the strength and personality of the out-of-phase leader. He may be far too interested in exercising power to take a back seat. His influence may be so strong that group members shift into his phase despite their natural inclinations.

If you're a member of a productive-phase group with this problem, there are a number of LIFE-CONTROL techniques that can save the day, things you can do either by yourself or in conjunction with your colleagues.

I've discussed these ideas in detail in the section on the introductory phase, but let me review them briefly here.

You and the other group members can:

• Try to ease the leader into production by following the natural path, by setting up a suitable structure, or by taking the smallest possible steps forward;
• Attempt to convince him to step aside temporarily and delegate the leadership; or
• Split into subgroups, with subgroup leaders appropriate to the work phase of their membership.

In each case, you and the other group members will be exercising the actual leadership. The leader may fight you all the way, so you'd better have a good understanding of where he is and where the group is.

If you're a leader who's in this situation, you have three alternatives: You can learn to be more flexible; allow or appoint someone to take over temporarily, until your phase and the group's match once more; or relinquish your leadership altogether.

Problems of membership

Once the productive phase is underway, there aren't likely to be any serious member problems, or at least few that originate with the members. In fact, only one category of membership problems is worth discussing at this point, out-of-phase members.

Let's start with the fellow who's an introductory phase-type and probably always will be. Instead of sticking to the plan, he'll be a constant source of upsetting new ideas and alternatives. He won't be interested in letting well enough alone. In a way, he'll be resistance-testing.

Let's say you've set up an evening at the theater with half-a-dozen friends. All arrangements have been made—the tickets have been purchased, the baby-sitters hired. Then, on the big night, one member of the group calls up and suggests bowling or miniature golf instead.

If you open up the idea for discussion again, you know there's going to be an empty row of seats at the theater and everyone will be out at least eight bucks. Worse yet, you all might wind up staying home, with nothing to entertain you but the re-runs.

The LIFE-CONTROL way to handle this is to let the person speak his piece, briefly. Then let him know what everyone else thinks, giving him no room for doubt. If you try to shut him up, he'll probably continue to spew out new ideas and you'll be lucky to carry out the original plan.

Another way to handle this person is to make use of his assets. Ask him to suggest an after-theater restaurant. Put him in charge of the next group outing. He's an idea man, remember. Find some way to use his originality.

The most troublesome type of member, as far as a productive-phase group is concerned, is the individual who's permanently in resistance-testing. If he's domineering and aggressive, he may appear to be engaged in open sabotage. If he's the quiet sort, his actions may seem like subversion.

This is the greatest threat from a member in resistance-testing in a group that's in its productive phase: his possible effect on others. If left alone or undisciplined long enough, he may gather allies from other anxious group members, splitting the organization into splinter groups. He may even throw the entire group headlong back into full-scale resistance-testing.

Faced with this kind of person in the group, the leader must act. If possible, the member should be seen for his assets rather than his liabilities. Characteristically, such people are good at finding flaws. For that reason, they can be useful as quality control inspectors, proofreaders, efficiency experts, etc.

If there's no way your group can use this individual's talents, you're going to have to give him some fairly firm guidance and direction. After all, that's what he's asking for.

You may have to tell him what rules apply, even if he's heard about them before. You may have to take him aside and make it very clear to him what he can and cannot do. You may have to set limits on him in some way.

If you do nothing, you'll be endangering the group and its goals in two ways: First, you'll be letting him continue on his present path, sowing disorder and disruption. Second, you'll be demonstrating your way of handling such problems and encouraging others to act up, since you don't seem to have the situation under control.

The way I've put it here, it may seem as though the group's official leader is the only one who can take action in this situation. Not so. Group members can accomplish the same thing, and in the same way. They can tell their erring colleague to cool it, with a fair chance of getting results. But, if they don't act as a unified body, the result may be more trouble, not less.

The other out-of-phase personality in a group that's well

into the productive phase is the termination phase-type. This person is in a hurry to get it over with. He wants to bring things to a end, so he can add to his storehouse of memories. His greatest satisfactions come from the past.

He's the diplomat who starts his autobiography before his last foreign assignment has come to an end, the chief clerk who spends the final six months before mandatory retirement saying his goodbyes and remembering—endlessly—the old days, the junior executive who buys an annuity at age twenty-eight.

Such people are usually harmless enough for a group that's in the midst of its productive phase. But they're not normally among the group's most productive members.

They present both a challenge and an opportunity: the challenge—to find the right slot for them, one consonant with their personalities; the opportuniy—to get even greater efficiency from the group.

As I've said, termination-type people, because of their natural interest in the past, are often good record keepers or historians. They often place great stock in a group's social aspects. They're often excellent on company newspapers, or turning out class bulletins, or at keeping everyone informed.

The key in any phase—and this is no less true in the productive phase than at other times—is to be aware of the inclinations of all the group members. And this is true whether you're a leader or a member. If you're a member, that knowledge will help you get along with your colleagues and help you influence them when that's what you want to do. If you're a leader, it will help you guide the group more surely toward its objective.

Problems of Circumstance

What happens to a group in the productive phase when something unexpected comes up—an interruption, a change in plans, an alteration of circumstances?

The answer is, not much. That's what the productive phase is all about, handling practical problems that occur in the course of accomplishing the stated objective. At least that's the case with all but the most severe problems.

Productive-phase groups often continue on, without pause, through a change in leadership, perhaps putting the new leader through a little resistance-testing when he takes over. Even families usually stay in the productive phase when the primary leader dies, if that's where they already were.

When Roosevelt died in the closing months of World War II, for instance, Hitler felt Nazi Germany had been delivered, that the Allied war effort would collapse without its leader. But that effort was firmly in the productive phase. Even though Truman was inexperienced and not well informed—at first—the Allies continued in the productive phase with hardly a pause.

There is one shift that can send a productive phase back to the beginning, however. That's the case when circumstances force a complete alteration in the original goal.

For instance, if husband and wife are both working, even moonlighting to keep up with inflation and put the kids through school, all will change if they should win the $100,000 state lottery. They'll have to go back to the beginning and devise a whole new productive-phase goal.

If the goal changes partially, though not entirely, the group may regress to the resistance-testing phase. If you and your family are driving out to see the Grand Canyon and you decide to stop off at Aunt Minnie's for a weekend, you can be sure you'll get some resistance-testing from the kids. Just how much depends on how far out of the way you'll be going.

If you're a salesman at Ajax Tool, with a quota of $50,000 worth of orders a month, and the word comes down from the top that you must henceforth produce $75,000 a month, the chances are you'll do a little resistance-testing before you accept the idea.

The applicable process rule here is: The greater the change, the greater the resistance-testing. This applies to the productive phase as well as the others. But groups in this part of the cycle have achieved considerable stability. It takes a lot more to upset them.

The Termination Phase

A Case History

On July 20, 1974, Arthur Green, president of Arthur Green and Son, Lumber and Hardware, placed an announcement in the *Courier-Telegram,* the local paper. It said that he was retiring from his firm as of August 1, after which his son Joe, long associated with the business, would be in charge.

In the normal course of events, Art Green probably would never have retired, even though he was sixty-seven years old. A big, vital, vigorous man who was liked even by his competitors, Green was a bear for work. He'd often demonstrated, proudly, that he was stronger than most men half his age.

But his doctors gave him no choice. After he'd had his first heart attack nearly three years ago, they'd ordered him to slow down, to little or no effect. In the previous winter, he had a second attack, more severe than the first. Recovery was uneventful, but his doctors told him that if he went back to work, even part-time, he'd be committing suicide.

Even so, Green was hesitant. His life was his work. He yielded, finally, but only after some high-powered persuasion from his son Joe and his daughter-in-law Lisa. Two arguments hit home: They pointed out that the little ones —Green's grandchildren, Melanie and Todd—had already lost Grandma Green (who had died five years earlier after a long illness). They needed to have their grandfather alive.

And they reminded Green that he had often said he intended to turn the business, just as soon as it was in good financial shape, over to Joe and go to a warm climate. Last year, Art Green and Son made more money than it ever had before, despite economic conditions. And this year looked even better.

Once he accepted the idea, Art Green seemed to take to it as if he were the one who'd thought it up in the first place. He started sending away for information about leisure and retirement communities located everywhere, from Florida to California. He talked about taking the trip to Europe he'd always dreamed of.

He considered all kinds of new ventures with which to occupy his time—carpentry, fishing, photography, and painting (all of which he'd dabbled in from time to time). He even hinted that he might not be immune to remarriage. "There's life in the old man yet," he'd say, with a wink.

Joe had hoped to get his father to stop coming into the store by the first of May, but Art wouldn't hear of it. There were still things to do. If he were going to turn the store over to his son, he wanted to be sure that nothing was left hanging, that no unexpected problems popped up after he began his retirement.

During May, June, and July, Joe found himself the sole student in an intensive, graduate-school level course in lumber and hardware retailing. His father literally taught his son everything he'd learned over the years. And though Joe had worked beside his dad for nearly a decade, ever since his house-building business had folded, he learned plenty.

In the middle of the summer, Art insisted that the two of them fly out to the Annual Lumber and Hardware Convention in Chicago. Art said he wanted to bid goodbye to all of his friends in the business.

That he did, talking about old times with everyone. But he also did the buying for the store one last time, continually instructing his son on how to get bargains and make deals. At the same time, he told all the manufacturers' reps about the management change at Arthur Green and Son.

In the first week of July, Art spent a few days in Arizona, buying a condominium. When he got back, he packed up his own place. He also wrote the announcement for the newspaper.

On July 30, the store employees held a party for "the boss," giving him a series of gag gifts and a very expensive camera. Art gave a little speech, telling everyone how he'd started the store nearly forty-five years ago from scratch and made it the success it was today. "I think I deserve a rest," he said. "I've done my job."

The next night, there was a family dinner at Joe's, with his older sister Elaine flying in from Wisconsin for the occasion. The family gave their father a set of interchangeable lenses, filters, carrying cases, etc., to go with the camera.

On August 1, Art gave his set of store keys to his son and boarded the noon plane for Tucson, after exchanging hugs and kisses with everyone. "Don't you worry about me," he told them. "I'm going to have the time of my life."

That night, he called, to tell them that he'd arrived safely. He also reminded Joe that Frank, the truckdriver, had asked for a day off, and said that the man deserved it. "Don't worry, Dad," Joe said. "I'll take care of it."

It was only the first of many such calls. They started at the rate of twice a wek or so and soon escalated to practically one a day, in combination with a letter or two each week.

Before he left, Art asked his son to send him copies of the newspaper ads. Now he was requesting copies of the monthly bank statements and even weekly sales figures, and giving detailed advice on the store's day-to-day operations.

Joe, who understood how much the business had meant to his father, decided to tolerate the old man's antics and even to respond to his requests, within reason. It seemed a small thing to do, even though the more Joe complied with his dad's requests, the more requests were made.

In Tucson, things weren't really going very well for Art Green. Within a month, he'd tried out all of the hobbies that interested him and found them boring. He made a few passing attempts to strike up friendships with his neighbors, managing to pick up a couple of golf partners but no more.

Art Green was depressed. He was restless. He was angry, but he couldn't have said why exactly. Even that European trip he'd long considered didn't excite his interest any more.

The weather was beautiful in Arizona but, except for an occasional walk to the grocery store and a golf game now and then, Green didn't take much advantage of it. Mostly he stayed home, studied the store's financial statements, watched TV, and wondered what to do with himself.

In the beginning of October, Joe and Lisa flew to Tucson with the kids. They'd intended to come earlier, but Joe had been unable to get away from the store.

Art was happy to see everyone. But after the amenities, when the kids were asleep, he had a thousand questions for Joe: Was the paint moving? Was the transmission on the delivery truck holding up? How was the new man working out? Did you bring the monthly statement?

Joe was ready for him. Everything was fine, he said, but he wasn't going to answer any more questions. He reminded his father that he'd retired. He also reminded him that he, Joe, was fully able to run things, maybe not as well as his father, but close enough.

Art Green got furious. He accused his son of cutting him out of the action, of being ungrateful, of not understanding his needs. He threatened to come back and take over again.

Joe just shrugged. If proving a point was good enough reason to die, he said, then there was nothing he could do about it. But as far as he was concerned, the old man was no longer going to be involved with the store. "I'm not even sure I'd tell you if we were going bankrupt, which, believe me, we're not."

Eventually, Joe was able to bring a philosophical tone to the argument. There comes a time in everyone's life, he said, when you have to let go. He said he knew it would come for him someday. But it was already here for his father. Besides, there was a whole new life out there, maybe better than the old one. However, there was no way to take advantage of it and also hold on to the past.

Art didn't like what his son was saying, but he knew Joe was right. Eventually, the old man stopped arguing and resigned himself to the fact that as far as the store was concerned he was out of business.

In the weeks that followed, Art did a lot of soul-searching. He wasn't a young man any longer. He didn't know how long he had to live. But he'd always been the sort to get the most out of what he had, whatever it was.

It was during this period that Art finally began to accept his new station in life. He looked back over his life, at his youth, at his middle years when he spent every moment he had at the store, at his heart attacks, and saw himself in a new light.

Not all people in Art Green's situation find something to do with their lives. Some just fade away. But Green wasn't the sort to do that. He took advantage of some bad luck that turned out to be good luck and found himself a new occupation.

It started on the golf course, near the eighteenth hole. Art lined up a long iron shot, swung and sliced the ball at almost a ninety-degree angle, and sent it crashing through the window of the maintenance building of the local community college.

To make a long story short, Art started talking to the maintenance man about what courses the school offered, what kind of people attended, etc. He wound up teaching three classroom hours a week—the subject was small-store retailing—and taking two different courses in photography.

Art went back to visit his family at Easter time. At the end of his first day there, which was unreservedly pleasant,

Joe took his father aside. We're thinking of taking over the vacant building next door and turning it into a garden shop, Joe said. He asked his father what he thought of the idea.

Art wryly raised an eyebrow, as if he were surprised to he consulted. It's an interesting thought, he allowed. He asked Joe to let him know what he decided, but *after* he made up his mind.

When last I heard about Art Green, he was working up a curriculum on small-store retailing and talking about going to a publisher with it.

The Essence of the Termination Phase

In the course of our lives, we all experience many termination phases. We graduate from school and start work. We forgo the single life and get married. We move from one house to another, from one city to another, from one job to another, sometimes from one spouse to another.

And eventually, no matter who we are, no matter what our circumstances, we come to the end of our own broad life cycle. For some people, that happens unexpectedly, as an interruption in the middle of some other life phase. For others—the majority, I think—it is a well-developed process unto itself.

Many groups also go through termination phases. Any group that's come together temporarily for the purpose of accomplishing a single task disbands automatically when its goal has been achieved. It goes through a termination phase. But so do some ostensibly stable and permanent groups such as families, businesses, schools, even nations. It all depends on circumstances—content.

Of all the phases in a cycle, termination may be the one that is most personal. True, termination does have a major impact on a group. It ends it. But that's mainly significant because of termination's effect on the individuals who comprise that group.

Termination phases accompany the completion of both

vital tasks and trivial ones. They can be essentially meaningless or intensely significant. They can affect millions of people—the termination of a war, for example—or just one.

In LIFE-CONTROL, however, it's the process that counts, not the content.

Four Miniature Phases in the Termination Phase

Even the termination phase, last in the cycle, can be subdivided into four smaller phases that recapitulate the entire process. Here's how they look:

1. *The introductory part:* This is when the idea is broached. Normally, termination phases are initiated by outside influences such as relocation, new opportunities, health changes, etc. Or, they come as a result of built-in limits such as deadlines met, tasks accomplished, jobs completed, enlistments up, terms over, and so on.

For an individual, the termination phase usually begins when he starts to recognize that he is completing the job, or when he realizes he might as well give it up (since he's not going to succeed or he's not interested in finishing), or when physical incapacity prevents him from continuing.

For a graduating college senior, for example, the approach of graduation is the initiating factor. But most seniors feel they've more or less accomplished what they've set out to do—go through four years of college, complete their education, and get their degree. They also see new projects ahead.

This combination of factors usually allows most seniors to begin the termination process with a positive attitude, which in turn allows them to experience a fully developed introductory part of the phase. The introductory part begins, as do all such periods, with the conceptualization of the idea, that the job at which the college student has been working at for four years is finally at an end, that the task has just about been completed. It is also characterized by excitement and even a touch of euphoria. The labors are over, a sometimes difficult task has been successfully accomplished, and a new time of life is about to start, one in which just about anything seems possible.

But, as the student gets into the introductory part of the phase, he may find that his initial conceptualization isn't quite accurate. The job isn't really finished, not to the last detail. There are tests to be taken, papers to be handed in, fees to be paid, books to be sold.

Most college seniors are able to buckle down during the last few months of school, to finish up these last details in good style. This is a responsible way to behave, since it insures that practical problems won't crop up to spoil the rest of the termination process.

2. *The resistance-testing part:* Resistance-testing is bad enough when it revolves around a new project. Change, we know, affects the group's and members' sense of security and stability. Nonetheless, this resistance-testing usually carries a promise of gain or reward, if the goal is reached.

The resistance-testing part of the termination phase, however, is not simply a time of change upsetting stability. It is also a time of great and apparently irretrievable loss.

Alice White had been planning her sweet sixteen birthday party for months, picking out decorations, figuring out whom to invite, planning what to wear, all with her mother's help. Then, with a rush, party night was upon her.

The party turned out to be a fabulous success. The games went off perfectly, everyone loved the food, and the presents were exactly what Alice wanted. But she didn't want the night to end.

Alice's parents had set eleven thirty as the end of the party, but at about eleven, Alice went to her mother and asked that the deadline be extended to twelve, "since everyone was having so much fun." Her mother hesitated, but finally agreed.

At about eleven thirty, Alice asked her mother if her five closest girl friends could sleep over. Mother and daughter had earlier agreed that the party wouldn't turn into an all-night event. This time, Mrs. White refused.

The young girl disappeared among the guests, then

reappeared a few minutes later. Could she go to sleep over at a friend's house, then? No, she could not, her mother said. Why not? Alice asked. Because she agreed to help clean up after the party, her mother told her.

Once more, Alice walked away, this time obviously sullen and angry. Her mother thought about what had transpired for a few minutes, then searched out her daughter. "I wouldn't object to a slumber party *next* weekend," she told the girl. Alice made a pretense of being still angry, but it was only a pretense. Before midnight, she had the next event all set up.

After the guests had gone Alice was very cooperative, as she'd promised.

The girl's original request to extend the party was typical resistance. She didn't want the event to end. Her mother —the leader, in this case—wisely bent, without breaking.

Alice's second request—for a slumber party immediately following the big event had clear-cut elements of testing. She wanted to know how far she could go in this situation. She wanted to see if her mother really had things, including Alice, under control.

During this period, the girl felt the anger, depression, and restlessness typical of a resistance-testing period. She wasn't at all sure she wanted to tolerate the feelings of loss when the party came to an end.

Like the good leader she was, Mrs. White finally established some limits. She made it clear to her daughter just what the rules were in this situation and what Alice could and could not do. And she did this without overreacting and forcing Alice to act up even more.

Once Alice saw that her mother had everything under firm control and could handle what was going on, she started to settle down. Her mother even wisely provided her with a way to cope with the feelings of loss that accompanied the end of the party—a new social event to anticipate.

3. *The productive part:* For the March of Dimes, the termination phase apparently began with the discoveries of Jonas Salk and Albert Sabin. Polio, the disease it had

been fighting all these years had been brought under control.

At first, after it became clear that its original goal had been accomplished, the people at the March of Dimes offices most likely felt the euphoria of the introductory phase, knowing that its aim had actually been achieved. Then there was probably the anger and depression of resistance-testing; this magnificent organization was about to be disbanded.

Then, obviously, came the productive phase. The board of directors of the charity stepped back from the situation, gained some perspective, and started applying what it had learned in the previous phases. It asked itself if it made sense to dissolve, to waste the skills and talents of the organization. And it asked itself how these skills might be utilized to a new end.

I'm sure there was a great deal of situational analysis going on at that time. The board was trying to figure out what came next, if anything. Finally, it developed another project worth doing, the funding of research in congenital disease.

This perpetuated the organization and put it back into a productive phase, while giving it a new goal similar enough to the old one that few major operational changes were needed.

Of course, the March of Dimes was fortunate. It was able to find a viable new project that made sense for it. Not all organizations are that lucky.

4. *The termination part:* For those individuals or organizations who actually must end their activity, whatever it was, this is the moment of leave-taking, the goodbye part.

It's usually not a difficult time or a complicated one, since most of the issues have been worked out in earlier parts of the phase. Very often, it's perfunctory, a transitional moment between one project and the next.

How does the termination part look? For an army unit disbanding, it's the time when bags are packed, when some soldiers take one last look at the barracks and the camp and others want nothing more than to take off as quickly as possible.

For a pro football team after winning the championship game, the termination part of the termination phase is when the last handshakes of congratulations are exchanged, when the last reporter has left, when the last player has changed into civilian clothing, when at last the event has come to its natural end.

Except at the very end of our lives—and often, even then—the termination phase of any one project is modified and softened by the fact that we're usually in other phases in other projects. In changing jobs, for example, we may go through a distinct termination phase while being in the productive phase of life, the introductory phase of a new hobby, the resistance-testing phase of a friendship, —whatever.

Even the area in which the termination phase is taking place is often modified by the nearly simultaneous beginning of an introductory phase (changing jobs is a good example).

This pattern also applies to many groups—businesses, schools, any organization that has not come together to perform a single task. And, the larger an organization or group is, the more likely it is to have multiple tasks. For that reason, it may be in the termination phase in one area, in resistance-testing in the introductory phase in another, etc. It may have dozens of projects in different stages.

All of these factors tend to smooth out the peaks and valleys in various groups activities, at least for the group as a whole. But, as I've said, the termination phase is intrinsically personal. So, whenever a person has a deep emotional investment in an activity and that activity comes to an end, he or she will be strongly affected.

Unique Problems

With the cycle coming to an end, it might seem as though opportunities for trouble within the group or concerning its stated task should be fading away. After all, the work is essentially done (successfully or not). The group is getting ready for other things. Its members are being released from their group obligations.

Well, in one sense, this notion is correct. The goal, first established in the introductory phase, has either been accomplished, partly accomplished, or given up. No longer must the group contend with the often-illusory excitements of the introductory phase, the conflicts of resistance-testing, or even the practicalities of production.

But, in many situations, for many groups and many members, oportunities for trouble still exist. Many projects can still turn sour in the termination phase at the very last minute.

For instance, if final details aren't attended to, some of the achievements or pleasures of the productive phase might be undone and some well-deserved rewards or satisfactions lost or diminished.

You and your family may have a glorious time touring the Greek islands, for example, but if you leave the suitcase with all of the souvenirs and the exposed film back at the hotel room when you fly home, some of the glow is sure to fade.

Or, if your group's project is one that interacts with other groups and other projects, they may suffer if your termination phase isn't handled properly.

You can imagine what might happen if the ground crew at a major airline didn't pass on its entire work schedule, along with all outstanding maintenance problems, when it went off shift and was replaced by the next ground crew. Because the result could be catastrophic, airlines have formal procedures to prevent exactly this occurrence.

Or, the project may go well enough, but some of the members might not come out of the termination phase in a position to go on to other things. They may have a great deal to give, because of their accumulated experience and knowledge, but nothing to which they can give it.

I saw a major tragedy of this sort occur when a famous

manufacturer of baked goods—cakes, pies, muffins, cookies, rolls, and such—unexpectedly went bankrupt last year, putting nearly one hundred skilled bakers out of work, many of whom had difficulty finding another job in their chosen field.

So there are some unique problems inherent in the termination phase, difficult problems that combine both content and process and require solutions of a similar blend.

The first of these problems occurs when the project comes to an end before it should, usually in the midst of the introductory part of the termination phase. I call it untimely termination.

The second takes place when, for any number of reasons, group members are never able to work through the issues inherent in termination. I call this problem inadequate closure. It's often caused by untimely termination.

Both can be very destructive, either to the group, its accomplishments, and other groups with which it interacts, or to its members, or both.

Then there's a third unique problem in this phase or, rather, a group of interrelated problems. They're all connected with a particular termination phase, the one that comes at the end of most people's lives.

Let's start with the first.

Untimely Termination

On June 5, 1968, Robert F. Kennedy was assassinated while campaigning in California for the Democratic Presidential nomination. Suddenly, the movement that had grown up around him, composed of politicians and a grass-roots following, existed only in memory.

The thousands of people who had worked for RFK and the millions who were hoping for a chance to vote for him were now left without a goal or purpose. They'd made anything from an emotional to an intellectual to a financial to a participatory investment in the RFK campaign. Now there was nothing.

Kennedy's death deprived these people from finishing what they'd started to do, from savoring their accomplishments (even coming close to the nomination would have been an accomplishment of sorts), and from productive participation in the Presidential campaign.

It visited on them not only the natural grief that comes with the death of a leader, but also a feeling of aimlessness, and of anger and frustration. And it eliminated the normal methods of discharging these emotions.

Some Kennedy partisans tried to attach themselves to other candidates such as McCarthy or Humphrey, but most did so half-heartedly. Others withdrew from Presidential politics, their disappointment too great for them to be able to carry on. And still others joined the antiwar demonstrators in Chicago, who, together with the police, provided a violent backdrop for the convention that nominated Humphrey.

As it happened, this untimely termination was caused by an outside circumstance, the assassination. But untimely terminations can have internal causes, too. These can occur, for example, when the president of a company has to call off a research project for lack of funds; or when a young girl falls out of love with her boyfriend just before the senior prom.

I've seen untimely termination strike all kinds of organizations, from small to large, devoted to business or to pleasure, in which members were getting monetary rewards or nothing but ego gratification.

I know of an instance in industry that should illustrate my point. It involved Dr. Karl Kresge (as we'll call him), a brilliant and well-known designer of jet aircraft.

Back in 1967, Wichita Aircraft Corp. (as we'll name it), a major manufacturer of business aircraft, decided it had to build and market a first-rate business jet if it were to keep up with its competitors.

But it had a problem. Its nine-man staff of engineers and designers, experienced and talented though they were, knew nothing about jets. In fact, they specialized in far smaller craft, single and twin-engine planes that seated anywhere from two to eight people.

Bill Abahazi, the new company president, formerly vice president of marketing at one of Wichita's competitors, thought he knew the perfect man for the job—Dr. Karl Kresge, the man responsible for the Starflight, the country's leading business jet, who was a NASA employee at the time.

Abahazi paid a visit to Kresge at Houston, offered him 30 percent more than NASA had been paying him and brought him back to Kansas. Kresge's assignment was simple: He was to produce a business jet prototype that could cruise at five hundred mph, with a range of three thousand miles and a payload of three crewmen and nineteen passengers, plus at least two thousand pounds of luggage.

Kresge took charge of the company's nine-man design team like a man with a mission. Within a few weeks, they were hard at work doing wind tunnel research, testing turbine blades for the engines, working with aluminum and titanium alloys, etc.

In about eighteen months, Kresge's group had produced working blueprints. Then they actually started fabricating the prototype aircraft, making use not only of Wichita's resources, but working with suppliers all over the country.

Every so often, Abahazi glanced through Kresge's progress reports or stuck his head into the design section to ask how it was going. The prototype was taking shape with reassuring speed.

On January 15, 1969, the first prototype of the Astrocruiser was rolled out of the firm's hangars and onto the Tarmac. With Abahazi, Kresge, and most of the rest of the company watching, the test pilot climbed in.

In a few moments, the engines were whining with that familiar note. Then the plane rolled down the runway, gathering speed. It swooped into the air impressively. After about a half-hour of stunning demonstration, it dropped out of the sky and made a perfect landing.

When Abahazi congratulated his designer, Kresge broke the news that he was returning to NASA in two weeks. The Government needed a man to help design the Space Shuttle, it seemed, and it was willing to pay for him.

Abahazi was upset at first, but then he realized that Kresge's departure might be a blessing in disguise. At least the company would no longer have to worry about his enormous salary.

About a month later, after some additional test flights, the pilot reported that the plane still had some minor bugs. The landing gear didn't always retract smoothly. There was some annoying and potentially dangerous vibration in one engine. The trim-tab in the rudder occasionally malfunctioned.

Abahazi called George Barkacs, who'd been Kresge's second-in-command on the design team, only to find he'd gone off fishing in Minnesota, intending to use up six weeks of accumulated vacation time. His assistant had gone with him. The rest of the team was confused and upset by Kresge's sudden departure.

Bill Abahazi spent the next week personally sorting out the many details that had been left unfinished in the design department. There were requisitions to be filled out and cost estimates to be refined. There'd been little liaison with materials acquisition. Public relations had scarcely heard of the new plane.

In the end, Abahazi was forced to go out and hire a new man to do what Kresge had left undone. He later estimated that Kresge's early departure cost Wichita Aircraft $1.3 million and three months of lead time, plus "I don't know how many orders."

It's true that if Kresge had stayed on, Wichita probably wouldn't have had as much trouble with the project. But the real fault lay with Bill Abahazi. He should have realized that Kresge would be moving on after the plane was wrapped up. Wichita Aircraft had nothing else to interest a man of his caliber.

Abahazi saw himself as a productive-phase leader, in a productive-phase company, an accurate view, as far as it went. But the Astrocruiser project was a separate subcycle within the company. It was destined to go all the way to termination, even though the company stayed in production.

Leaders' Responsibilities

Leaders in the termination phase have a number of responsibilities, many of which Abahazi forgot or didn't understand:

- They must reinforce a job well done, so that group members will get satisfaction from their work and maintain a sense of group identity.

From the start, Abahazi had a problem with Kresge and group identity. The designer saw himself as an itinerant scientist, traveling from project to project, from company to company. It was this attitude, in fact, that led him to leave the company so quickly.

To hold on to him, at least until the termination phase was completed, Abahazi should have more clearly spelled out his responsibilities from the first. He should have shown Kresge just what the plane meant to the company and how much his contribution was valued. He should have done everything possible to make the man an integral part of the group.

- They must coordinate with the next cycle or with other systems whose work depends on the group that's coming to the termination phase.

Abahazi should have realized that Kresge was an airplane designer, pure and simple. He shouldn't have expected the man to be interested in budgets, requisitions, raw materials, and public relations. It was his responsibility to make sure nontechnical details were handled properly, not Kresge's.

It was also his responsibility to make sure there was a second-in-command who could take over after the prototype had been produced, to work out bugs and to prepare the plane for mass production.

- They must prepare for systematic closure.

The best way to make sure that everything gets done once a group enters its termination phase, to make sure that all loose ends are tied off, that nothing is left hanging, that secondary groups are properly informed, that conditions are set up so that the next cycle can begin smoothly, is to create a structure.

This structure can be anything that's convenient, a check list, a flow chart, a careful and explicit division of responsibilities, or a set of blueprints. But it should include every last task the group must do, down to the last item in the termination part of the termination phase.

Bill Abahazi made no real effort to create such a structure, or if he did, he didn't make it known. If he had, Wichita Aircraft might have weathered Kresge's departure without a quiver.

If Abahazi had attempted to view the process aspects of the project instead of concentrating entirely on content, he could very easily have avoided any difficulties.

This story I relate is not so unusual. Businessmen, even those in very high positions, are human. They make human mistakes, of the sort we all make from time to time, even if we supervise no one. Only the content is really different.

Bill Abahazi lost control of his situation for the same reason most of us lose control. We don't look at process. We're too consumed with content. We think if we can only master the events of our lives, we'll be all right.

The truth is, we must master both the events and their meaning, in the broadest sense. That's the essence of LIFE-CONTROL, the single principle that matters most.

Inadequate closure

Untimely termination takes place when the cycle is truncated and important matters are left undone. Inadequate closure, on the other hand, can take place when something goes wrong, when there is untimely termination, or when everything goes according to schedule.

In this circumstance, the group can accomplish its goal, tie up all loose ends, coordinate with other groups or systems that might be affected, and even prepare others to take over where the original group had left off—and still leave a serious, potentially tragic problem unsolved. The problem is how to rescue group members from their sense of loss and guide them toward rewarding new activities.

There's a case history in my files that illustrates this difficulty. It involves a young man I'll call Jim Dobbins, who left Monroe High School in the suburbs of a large, metropolitan city about four months before he was due to graduate. His father, an oil company executive, had been reassigned to Venezuela by his firm.

Mrs. Dobbins arranged with the school to have her son tutored in his classes until he completed the assigned work. His final exams and essays were to be sent back and graded. If he passed—and everyone was sure he would, since his grades had always been fairly good—the school would send him his diploma.

Jim had been a fairly happy-go-lucky boy before he left Monroe High. He'd dated frequently and had many male friends. He'd been active in extracurricular activities, taking part in the class play, serving on the student council, and playing junior varsity basketball.

But, within a few weeks after arriving at his new home, all of that changed. He had nothing to do with his spare time, now that he had no school activities. He wrote a couple of letters to some friends, but stopped when he realized his chances of seeing them again were slim.

As time wore on, Jim became sullen, withdrawn, and uncharacteristically irritable. He let his studies slide. He spent a great deal of time in his room with his door closed, saying nothing to his family.

His mother managed to get him to finish his schoolwork though, in truth, she did half of it herself. When his diploma arrived, Jim took one look at it and stuck it into a closet.

Jim had never been interested in going to college. He'd always talked about working for the oil industry, out in the field. That summer, his father got him a job on a rig. He held it for only a few weeks. Then his father found him a position at the pumping station. Jim blew that one, too.

What finally happened to Jim Dobbins, I do not know, though I could hazard a guess. I do know, however, the main reasons for his unhappiness.

Because of his incomplete closure from high school, Jim Dobbins found himself with intense feelings of loss he could not deal with. He was unable to put things into perspective, to assimilate what had happened to him and go on to other things.

But let's look at the senior year of Dean Flanagan, one of Jim Dobbins's classmates.

At Monroe High, all seniors must participate in a program known as Future Planning. For those going to college, this is when applications are filled out and recommendations obtained. For those going directly into the workaday world, there are individual sessions with the guidance counselor, plus aptitude and preference tests.

Dean Flanagan, who wasn't much of a scholar, took the tests, and discovered that his interests and abilities coincided. He loved working wih engines and he had a definite knack for things mechanical, which he'd already discovered in shop class.

It wasn't long afterward that his guidance counselor told him that a foreign-car repair shop nearby wanted some part-time help. Would he be interested? He was. As a result, he soon found himself with an after-school job, one that even had a future.

Meanwhile, the pace quickened at school. Teachers began to give out final assignments and ask for final papers. Work was fast coming to an end. At the same time, the social pace was picking up.

Most of the students now had dates for the senior prom

and were busy buying formals or renting tuxedos. They were also getting themselves fitted for caps and gowns for the graduation ceremony.

Toward the end of May, the yearbooks came out. Everyone, especially the seniors, had his friends and even teachers sign up. By this time, most of those who had applied to college had received acceptances. And a number of people, Dean Flanagan included, had made employment plans. Dean had been asked by the repair shop to begin working full-time after he was out of school.

Finally, after a flurry of last-minute studying, the teachers gave the final exams. It was downhill from that moment on. The senior prom took place that weekend. The next Wednesday, the final grades were released.

On the next Sunday, the three hundred graduating seniors, their parents and relatives, and many members of the school administration and faculty attended graduation ceremonies.

The speaker was Lawrence Heginbotham, president of First Federal Bank and former city mayor. His address consisted of well-worn platitudes, but it was well received nonetheless.

That night, and for most of the next twenty-four hours, graduation parties abounded, complete with casks of beer, loud music, and dancing, plenty of carousing and pranks. At one party, the students made an effigy of George Dettinger, the high school principal, and threw it into the swimming pool, but there was no serious misbehavior.

After a two-week vacation, Dean Flanagan began full-time employment at Carlin's Foreign Car Repair. He stayed there for three years. When last I heard of him, he was chief mechanic for the City Line Bus Company, a good, stable job. And he was married to Karen McElroy, a girl he'd dated in school.

All of this may sound like a typical senior year at a typical Midwest high school, which it was. But it is also a textbook example of how inadequate closure can be avoided by means of LIFE-CONTROL.

Let's take a look at what happened from the process viewpoint:

First, the leadership—the school administration, represented by the guidance counselor—involved group members (senior students) in a formal articulation program. This program had a single object, to prepare them for the new cycle that would begin following the termination of the present cycle.

For the same reason, the military services have mustering-out programs, in which draftees or enlisted men being returned to civilian life are first taught that they're no longer soldiers, then given help deciding on what they're going to do on the outside. Some prisons have similar programs.

Attempts at articulation are the leadership's recognition of its responsibilities, not only to the group and its goals, but also to the members as individuals.

Second, the school conducted a systematic closure procedure—final papers, final assignments, final tests, etc. Everything took place in an ordered, step-by-step manner, preserving stability and security throughout the phase and making certain that all last-minute details were properly handled.

This is what astronauts do as they return from a space venture. They go through a check list point by point, flipping switches, reading gauges, performing final tasks. (And it was when this procedure wasn't fully carried out during the final moments of the Apollo/Soyuz space shot, just before splashdown, that the American crew inadvertently gassed itself.)

Third, recognition was given for work well done. As the tasks came to an end, rewards and certificates were handed out and final grades were posted. Then, at graduation ceremonies students got the ultimate recognition—the culmination of twelve years of schooling—a diploma and public congratulations.

This is analogous, of course, to the notorious gold watch that's given to retiring employees after thirty years or so on the job. But the gold watch, in process terms, is not a good choice of reward. If there's one thing retiring employees don't need to know, it's what time it is.

Fourth, group members were given an opportunity to gain their own sense of completion, through a series of parties that began with the senior prom and ended with graduation-night beer blasts.

In our society, formal parties—be they birthday parties or New Year's Eve parties or anniversary parties—usually signify both the completion of one cycle and the beginning of another. Therefore, they're particularly apt during the high school graduation period.

Fifth, all of the events were surrounded by and infused with tradition. Tradition is one of our most powerful sources of security and stability. That's why the song of the same name in *Fiddler on the Roof* rings so true.

"How do we keep our balance?" Tevye sings. "That I can tell you in one word, tradition. Because of our traditions, everyone here knows who he is and what God expects from him. Without our traditions, our life would be as shaky as a fiddler on the roof."

Practically everything the Monroe High School graduating class did was swathed in tradition, since graduating classes had been doing all these things for years, even for generations. (And there is every reason to expect they will keep doing them.)

The moment of most intense tradition was the graduation ceremony itself, with not only the graduates but much of the community participating. Few events are more traditional than the handing-out of diplomas and the commencement speech.

That speech represents the essence of stability, delivered as it usually is by a town leader who symbolizes stability. Even the speech itself is normally traditional in content. People expect certain things to be said and they usually are.

These traditional exercises are aimed mainly at the graduating seniors, but they also have a reinforcement effect on the entire community. After all, those graduates represent the infusion into the community of new vitality, new ideas, new generations.

The system provided for reminders and follow-up. The end of every cycle, even when it hasn't been entirely pleasant, is accompanied by feelings of loss on the part of the group members.

Come fall, or come next year, or come five years from now, Dean Flanagan and all the other members of his graduating class will feel a certain emptiness when they realize they're not going to be returning to the old stomping grounds. Even those who are occupied productively with other ventures will feel a pang now and then.

The problem here is loss—of friends, of associates, of good times, of unlimited options, of innocence, of youth, and the like. Of course, this loss is never complete. At the least, memories remain. And most group members will have taken away other things from the experience—knowledge, skill, emotional growth and development, etc.

But, when the pain is acute, they'll all have a collection of artifacts to reassure them that in a sense the experience is still with them—yearbooks, class rings, prom programs, pressed corsages, class pictures, etc.

In addition, there will doubtless be further follow-ups over the years. For those graduating seniors who remain in the community or who can make it home, there will be a homecoming game and dance each fall.

For those who don't, there will be other follow-ups over the years, as a reunion committee inevitably forms, sends out a bulletin or newsletter, and holds anniversary parties.

All of these things ameliorate the loss and help the members assimilate the change they've experienced.

Let's go back to Jim Dobbins for a moment (the boy who moved to Venezuela). If his parents and guidance counselor had understood the precepts of LIFE-CONTROL, if they'd been aware of the process he was going through, they might have been able to help him adjust to his new situation.

For instance, they might have delayed their move or allowed him to join them later, or sent him back for the final week. If that were impossible, they might have made sure he went through Future Planning before he left, and given him a graduation party before the move.

You might think that I've picked an insignificant example to illustrate this section. There are, I'll admit, far more profound terminations than high school graduation. But for almost everyone, this is one of our first major terminations of any substance. How we deal with it may affect us for the rest of our lives.

At any rate, the principles I've delineated apply to termination phases of whatever content. They all require some sort of articulation program, some sort of closure.

For instance, I once witnessed a sales meeting in which the president of the firm was describing the company's new line to his sales force in glowing terms. He had them on the edge of their chairs. Then, just as he was coming to his close—he'd promised to give them a sales slogan that would really work—he was called away from the rostrum because of an emergency back at the plant. The salesmen just milled around after he left, frustrated and restless.

The president returned the next day, recapped his sales pitch, and told the men about the new slogan. The salesmen's enthusiasm was rekindled. A good leader can always rejuvenate the group's interest in a project.

To give another example, I think we've all had the feeling of inadequate closure when we've walked out of a very exciting movie with an equivocal end, where we didn't definitely know the fate of the main character, with whom we'd gotten very involved.

The Termination Phase of Life

In our society, the termination phase of life and the concept of dying are too often synonymous. As a result, many people spend their "declining years" simply waiting for the end.

The ideal, from the LIFE-CONTROL point of view, is to extend one's productive phase for as long as possible and, hopefully, to be in the midst of it at death.

We all know people, though probably too few, who have started new careers after they've retired, or who have gotten involved in rewarding projects, or who have taken on important new family roles.

These people have demonstrated their understanding of the notion that rewards and accomplishments need not come to an arbitrary end with the beginning of life's termination phase.

If people in this phase are aware of their unique assets, their knowledge of life and their perspective, they can often find ways to exercise leadership over their lives, to regain or maintain control over the satisfaction they receive from life.

I know of one remarkable woman who did this under the most difficult circumstances of life, after she'd been told she had only a few months to life.

Frances Miller (as I'll call her) was an extraordinarily energetic and vital woman in her late sixties. She was married to a retired restaurant owner, had two grown, married children and three grandchildren.

When her doctor first broke the news to her, she went through a classic introductory phase, in which she almost euphorically claimed she'd beat the disease no matter what the doctor had said. Of course, she hadn't really come to terms with her illness. She didn't believe she was going to die.

But her condition grew worse. It began to be obvious that she was not gaining in her struggle to live. Finally, she accepted her doctor's verdict, an act analogous to the commitment a group makes at the end of the introductory phase.

Then Mrs. Miller promptly went into a period of resistance-testing. She was angry that this was happening to her. She wasn't ready to die. She complained about her symptoms. She didn't take medication on time. Her usual calm acceptance of life was replaced by a constant irritability that could only partly be explained by her physical discomfort.

Then she fantasized that if she did her part by taking all her medicine, she would get better. When she finally realized the reality of her illness, she became very depressed.

But, as I've said, Frances Miller was an extraordinary woman. She somehow came to terms with the fact that she hadn't much longer to live. And she decided to do what she could with the weeks she had left. Her attitude of calm stability returned, with a surprising new note, a touch of humor.

For the nevt five weeks, even while her health visibly deteriorated, Mrs. Miller set out to help her family and friends adjust to her coming death. She refused to let them hold out hope for a miracle and she refused to keep the subject quiet. She insisted in talking about what she was experiencing, to anyone who would listen.

Her message was that death really wasn't all that bad, at least not for someone who had lived as full a life as she had. It was a natural conclusion to life that was neither good nor bad. It was another experience, another opportunity to grow and learn, until the very last moment.

To be sure, what was happening to her was no laughing matter. But neither was it a subject for copious crying and bereavement. She did her best to make those who visited her comfortable by saying what they were too embarrassed to say.

At the same time, she reviewed the best times of her life, the moments of greatest joy and satisfaction. She shared her vivid memories with her family and friends, almost as if she were turning these memories over to their safekeeping. Actually, she was giving family and friends—and herself—a sense of closure and completion.

She kept this up as long as she could, simultaneously staying off pain-killing drugs so that her mind would be as clear as possible. But finally she knew she must have them. The productive part of the termination phase had ended.

For the next few days, I understand, she entered a time of ethereal peacefulness. She wasn't a very religious woman, so she didn't think much about God. But she told her family she felt a profound oneness with the universe.

Frances Miller had made up her mind to control her life, even at its very end. And she was determined enough, and in good enough mental and physical condition, to devise her own closure program and follow it.

I'm not saying everyone can do this. She was an unusual woman. But, if she could do it, so can many others—especially those who have not just weeks to live, but years.

Part of the responsibility here lies with the group, society in this case. It needs as many productive members as possible. And it can ill afford to prematurely lose those who may be among its most valuable, those people in the termination phase of their lives.

No doubt instinctively, society (assisted by circumstances) is beginning to follow some LIFE-CONTROL precepts in regard to these members. The idea of mandatory retirement is slowly fading. And more and more industries are offering early retirement so employees can get started on another career.

In addition, human longevity is gradually increasing and most of us are staying healthier longer.

Combined, these factors are extending the productive phase of life for most people, a very desirable goal from both society's point of view and from the individual's.

But one only has to briefly contemplate our nation's old-age homes to realize that this trend hasn't gone nearly far enough.

For their sake and ours, our elders need a systematic closure program, one that gives them both a sense of completion and a sense of accomplishment.

They need to be honored and recognized for their achievements.

They need contact with others, to diminish their sense of loss, and not just with those who share their life phase.

Most of all, they need articulation program that will help

them deal with the problems inherent in the termination phase and simultaneously lead them into new cycles and new phases that will extend their productive lives almost until the last moment, if possible.

For society, the LIFE-CONTROL way to provide these needs is to find ways that better use our elders' greatest assets—their perspective, their powers of reflection and observation, their knowledge of life.

Oriental societies do this very well already. Their elders are revered and honored. To a lesser degree, the West does the same thing. Many of our judges are older people. And our elder statesmen are just that.

Obviously, we can't make all of our elders into judges or statesmen. But we can do a lot better at finding tasks for them that make use of their unique assets.

For example, one of the cities in which I consult—Newark, Delaware—is bringing grandparents into the elementary schools to help teach the children, random grandparents unrelated to anyone in the class. The school administration structures the situation and instructs the grandparents so that the necessary material gets taught in the necessary period.

I've seen this in action and, let me tell you, it's a natural. The kids love the grandparents and the grandparents love the kids. More than that, the children respect the grandparents and the grandparents have an unusual sensitivity to the children and their problems.

Many of our major cities have another sort of program to put our senior citizens to productive work and to make use of their special skills, something usually called the Executive Job Corps.

These organizations are usually composed of retired businessmen. Their purpose is to advise younger businessmen, often people who are just getting started. It's an excellent way to put the perspective and experience of our elders to work, for their benefit and for the benefit of others.

A society fully aware of the process involved in the termination phase will devise more programs like these.

It will recognize the assets of those facing the termination phase and put them to good use, helping them begin new productive cycles.

This is LIFE-CONTROL on the broadest scale, with the broadest benefits.

General Problems

The termination phase, as I've said, can be the most personal of all the phases. If the work is truly finished, it matters less what happens to the group as a group. Its reason for existence has ended. What counts now is what happens to the group members, and, of course, what happens to the completed task.

(Of course, a group may find a way to extend its work, or it may come up with a new project altogether. In that case, either a subcycle has been terminated or a new major cycle begins.)

I've already discussed most of the process issues that can affect a group member at this point—matters of closure, articulation, recognition, loss, etc.

But there are some general difficulties that may also impinge on the member's satisfaction and happiness. They're the same trio that affect other phases:

- Leadership problems in which the group members are faced with either an absent leader, or one who overreacts to testing, or one who is out of phase;
- Membership problems in which the group must deal with members who are out of phase; and
- Problems of circumstance, external events that affect the group in some unexpected way.

Because work-associated problems are mainly solved by this time, most of these general difficulties are less troublesome than in other phases. Still, they're worth talking about because of their effect on group members.

We'll start at the beginning.

Leadership Difficulties

Leaders in the termination phase have two sorts of responsibility:

First, they're responsible to the original objective. They must oversee the completion of all final details, coordinate the group's activities with other groups that might be affected, and prepare others to take over when that fits the circumstance. In short, they must do what they can to preserve and protect the group's accomplishment. They must prevent premature termination, if possible.

Second, they're responsible to the group members, whether or not they're aware of it. They should see to it that the members get the recognition they deserve, that they have a sense of completion, that they are prepared to go on to something new. They should do everything possible to prevent inadequate closure.

Yet, there are external factors and accidents of personality that can make the fulfillment of those responsibilities that much more difficult during the termination phase, even if the leader is aware of them.

1. *Absence or withdrawal:* Like the resistance-testing phase, the termination phase is a time of change. The job is over. What will follow it may be a matter of uncertainty. Group members are bound to feel a sense of loss, even if the cycle has had its unpleasant moments.

In this situation, the leader's responsibility is to provide security and stability. And there's no way he can do that if he isn't on the scene and active. He should certainly be there during the introductory and resistance-testing parts of the phase. After that, once the members are in the productive part, the adjustment has taken place. The members have become their own leaders.

2. *Overreaction.* Because members feel a great deal of anxiety because of the approaching change in this phase, resistance-testing may be fierce. The leader should do his best to recognize it for what it is—not a personal attack or

a judgment directed at him, but an expression of anxiety, a request for guidance and reassurance.

If he is to maintain the stability and security the group needs to finish those final practical details, the leader must not overreact to any testing that comes his way. If he does, he may cause the job to be left partially incomplete. And he may make it that much more difficult for the members to accept the project's end and come to terms with it.

3. *Out-of-phase leaders.* If, in its termination phase, a group finds itself with a leader who knows what must be done before the job is complete, who has the strength to provide the necessary security for the group members, who is willing to admit it when the job is done, and who has the sensitivity to be aware of his responsibilities to the members afterward, it can hardly ask for more.

But a group in the termination phase could very easily find itself with a leader whose temperament doesn't match its situation.

For example, a termination-phase group might discover that its leader is basically an introductory phase-type, someone whose main interest is in new ideas, not in the last details of old ones.

I once knew such a man at an advertising agency. A creative, innovative individual, he'd fire off new ideas by the minute. But he was impatient while they were being turned into print ads or TV commercials. He'd often pull his best men off a project before it was finished and start on a new one.

Or, a termination-phase group might come to realize that its leader is a resistance-testing-type, a law-and-order man in a time when there isn't much left to regulate.

I heard of a Boy Scout leader with this sort of temperament. He led his forty-man troop on a fifteen-mile march one summer, followed by three nights in the woods. Then he marched the boys back to town. Their parents were waiting for them, but he wouldn't release the boys until the bugler, who was limping in a couple of miles behind everyone else, arrived and sounded the retreat.

Or, a termination phase group might discover it has a leader who's really a productive phase personality, a man well qualified to get the job done, but not so well qualified to take care of the human aspects of the group.

I had an English teacher like this once, who was determined to have us read every last chapter of our required reading, no matter what. Two days before the semester ended (and with it, her class), she assigned us *Julius Caesar*. And I think she actually expected us to read it.

A reasonably strong group in the termination phase may be able to complete its work satisfactorily under any one of these leaders, since there is so little work to do by this time, and since the members may be still at least partially in a productive mood.

If the group is reasonably responsible, it may be able to overlook the impatience of an introductory phase-type leader and complete the final details, then use his enthusiasm and new ideas to gain momentum for a new cycle.

The resistance-testing and productive phase-type leaders will see to it that the job gets done, but they may overlook the emotional needs of the members. Whether or not the members can take care of these needs by themselves depends on many factors.

If you're a member of a termination-phase group led by a resistance-testing-type, you and your colleagues can use the applicable LIFE-CONTROL principles to right the situation:

- Try to ease the leader into termination by suggesting a suitable structure, in this case a systematic closure;
- Attempt to convince him to delegate the leadership to someone more in tune with the group; or
- Split into subgroups, with subgroup leaders appropriate to termination-phase tasks.

In the case of the resistance-testing-type leader, you'll have a difficult task on your hands, since he'll tend to categorize any of these attempts as a challenge to his authority.

The production phase-type leader, however, may be amenable to suggestions of systematic closure, if such suggestions can be put into the productive framework. Make him realize that guiding the members through closure and toward a new cycle is part of the original task.

If you're an out-of-phase leader in charge of a termination-phase group, you can try to empathize with the members and act accordingly, or allow or appoint someone to take over. This may not be so difficult, since the task is essentially accomplished.

Membership Problems

Most membership problems have been discussed in the section on unique phase problems, but one type of problem member remains, the out-of-phase member. Of the three personality types who might be out of phase in a termination-phase group, the member who's basically a resistance-testing-type may present real problems, to the group as well as to himself.

An introductory-phase member in a group of this sort is in a good position to start thinking about a new cycle, and perhaps to interest others in a new project he's thought of. The only difficulty, and it's a minor one, is to make sure he sticks around long enough to do his job.

A productive-phase member will also be ready to move on, to extend the project, or to find a new one to work on. The only problem he might present is an unwillingness to stop work, a certain obsessiveness more damaging to himself than to the group. Leaders and other members should be particularly sensitive to this person's needs. If possible, they should help him start a new cycle, to minimize his frustrations.

A member whose basic personality is of the resistance-testing variety could be destructive during the termination phase. He could make it difficult for the group to complete its final task. He could exacerbate other members' feelings of disconnection and loss by attacking any new projects that are suggested.

At a restaurant one night, I saw just such a man sitting with a group of his friends at the next table.

Everyone in his party had had a good time and was starting to feel sorry the evening was coming to an end. But he persistently shot down every attempt to suggest something the group might do together on the next weekend.

Finally, one woman in the group turned to him and said, with a very sweet smile, "Well, now it's your turn to suggest something, Harry. What would you like to do most? Don't tell me you'd rather watch TV and turn in early."

Harry gulped, protested that he didn't have any new ideas to offer, and never opened his mouth again while the rest of the group planned an evening at the theater, including him.

I think that woman handled him perfectly. She let him know, without insulting him, that he always had the option of bowing out, if that's what he really wanted. She also let him know that he'd been negative long enough, that it was his turn to be positive.

In a more formal group, if you're the leader, you may have to tell this member that the rules still apply, even in the termination phase. You may have to discipline him in some way.

If you don't, you'll be endangering the growth and development of the other group members. At this period, they need all the security and stability they can get, so they can start thinking about new cycles.

If the problem isn't too serious, a member who understands what's going on and who has the respect of the other members may be able to take over this job from the leader. But if the resistance-testing-type persists or his acting up intensifies, only the man at the top will be able to handle him. And, for the sake of the group, he'd better.

Problems of Circumstance

What happens to a group in termination when the unexpected occurs?

That depends, both on the content of the circumstance—good news, bad news, or simple interruption—and the part of the phase the group is in.

Let's say it's bad news. The group has been terminated suddenly and without warning instead of after a decent interval, as had been expected.

If the group is in the introductory part of the phase, there'll be trouble, both for the group and its job and for its members. Everyone will experience untimely termination and inadequate closure. The job will never be completely finished. The group members will wander away, wondering what to do next.

An example stands not two miles from my home. It's a fourteen-story apartment building without windows, without electrical service, without finished interiors. It seems that the developers ran out of money before the building could be finished. It's obvious what that circumstance did to the project. And you can guess how the workers reacted when, after coming to the site one day, they found their jobs no longer existed.

If the group is in the resistance-testing part of the phase, there'll still be trouble, but the group members will suffer more than the project, since it will usually be pretty well buttoned up by this time. Resistance-testing is the time when group members are still trying to deny that change is to take place. They're struggling to adjust. Sudden termination makes that more difficult.

An example? Well, think of a fourteen-year-old boy and a thirteen-year-old girl, coming home from what is their first unchaperoned date. He's taken her to her doorstep and is working up the courage to give her a kiss. She's working up the courage to accept it. At precisely the moment he bends forward, her mother opens the door and says, "Cynthia, I'm glad you're home. Say good night to the young man now and come in."

But the effects of a "bad news" interruption drop off dramatically when the group in termination reaches the productive part of the phase, or when it comes to actual termination.

By this time the group members have come to terms with the change they're undergoing. They've regained their sense of continuity. They have the entire cycle in perspective.

So, if there's a sudden termination, for example, they accept it without much fuss.

Now, what about good news—an extension of the productive phase, for example? You'd probably guess that good news wouldn't be much of a problem, and you'd be right. But, if it happens late in the phase, it may mean the beginnings of a whole new cycle.

I know of a young man, for instance, who applied to the graduate school of his university some months before graduating, but went through commencement ceremonies without getting word one way or another. He was disappointed, but he went home and started looking for a job. He'd accepted the idea that he wasn't going any further in school. Then, on August 15, just before going to work for a local firm, he got word that he'd been accepted, after all. He went back to school that fall as if he were starting all over again.

Okay. Now, how about interruptions?

These may be disconcerting and confusing during the introductory part of the phase and they may extend resistance-testing. They should be avoided for that reason, if at all possible. But they won't have much of an effect on the latter part of the phase.

There's more I could say about the termination phase, and about each of the earlier ones. But you now have a good understanding of the basic theory. Let's get on to some ways you can put it to more use in your own life.

Using
LIFE-CONTROL

In this book, my sole aim has been to teach you the principles of LIFE-CONTROL in such a way that you can apply them to your own life, to gain (or regain) mastery over those areas that more and more seem beyond your control.

My plan has been to dissect the phases that every task-oriented group, its leadership and its members, go through on the way toward their goal; to show you the process that occurs, regardless of content.

By now, I think you have a pretty good understanding of the four phases, their four miniature parts, the unique and general problems that can crop up in each phase, and the ways both leaders and members can deal with these problems.

But the true test of any theory is how it works in real life. In the preceding pages, I've tried to illustrate the process issues with a great many case histories from my files and from my own experience.

Real life—your life—starts out with content, however. So, in this final section, I intend to take a number of common, everyday questions I've been asked by people grappling with the content of their lives, analyze them according to LIFE-CONTROL precepts, and give LIFE-CONTROL solutions.

My hope is that this approach will be helpful to you. Though the problems I deal with on the following pages may differ slightly in detail from your own experiences, I think they'll be the sort of situations you find yourself confronting on a day-to-day basis.

By the time we come to the last of the questions, I hope and trust, you'll be able to examine the fabric of your own life from the process viewpoint and apply LIFE-CONTROL solutions to the difficulties you face.

My fiancée is telling me she isn't sure about getting married now, though she claims she loves me as much as ever. The wedding is only a week off and I'm getting frantic. What should I do? Will things be okay if we get married?

What's probably going on here, from the process viewpoint, is that the bride-to-be is going through the resistance-testing part of the introductory phase. After the initial excitement, the doubts and fears have started to surface. They may peak just before the wedding.

What you should do, in this situation, is reassure her that these feelings are common, that they're bound to occur. Chances are that if you don't panic and can show her you're in control, she'll be able to weather her doubts.

Incidentally, you should expect to feel some of these doubts yourself. Resistance-testing is inevitable in every phase. She may wind up having to reassure you.

As for whether these doubts mean your marriage may not be a good one, that's impossible to say. Everyone has doubts, yet some people have good marriages. I can assure you that you will probably have a pleasant honeymoon period, unless the doubts are too strong to overcome and the wedding never takes place. Resistance-testing often reaches a peak just before a productive period.

I hate to fire people, but there's this guy who works for me who is disrupting the whole business. I'm pretty sure he isn't even honest. What should I do with him?

Fire him, no matter how hard it is. Or, get the second-in-command to fire him if you must. If you don't take action, he'll seriously damage your organization.

First, his actions will disrupt business. Second, your lack of action against him will seem like permissiveness to others, who may wind up copying his behavior. Third, you will use him as a scapegoat. When the leader feels uncomfortable about something or someone, so will the group members.

Remember, the group is almost always more important than any single member. Firing the man may make you extremely uncomfortable, but if you don't, the consequences may be severe.

Can you put Ford's Presidency in LIFE-CONTROL *terms?*

It seems to fit, so far. When Nixon resigned and Ford took over, he went through an introductory phase with Congress and the country that had all the earmarks of a honeymoon. Then, about the time he pardoned Nixon, the resistance-testing phase began. Congress wasn't so cooperative. His popularity dropped suddenly. That phase apparently came to an end with the Mayagüez incident, in which Ford demonstrated his leadership capacities.

I'd say he's in the productive phase now. Of course, there are problems. There always are in the productive phase. But they're largely practical. No one is questioning Ford's leadership any more, and you hear very little talk about his being the first American President not elected to national office.

As for the termination phase, the jury is still out on that one. It may begin with the coming election campaign or it may not. But it's no surprise to me that he's running for re-election. He's trying to extend his productive phase, like any sensible person.

I'm worried about this women's lib business. My wife is going to these meetings and she's upsetting our whole relationship. I don't see how the family can survive it, as an institution. Will families still exist when my kids are old enough to get marred?

Yes. The family is the molecular unit of society. It's the model for all other groups and the training ground for members and leaders. What's changed in recent years is the extended family, which has withered considerably, leaving the nuclear family with less stability and security than before, and in a time of increasing need due to the pressures of modern life.

There are only three possible ways the nuclear family could strengthen itself. First, the man could take an even more dominant role. That's clearly impossible. Second, the children could take part in the leadership. Very unlikely, I think. Third, the woman could exercise greater strength and become a full-time co-leader.

This is the change that's taking place now, I believe. And it has the additional bonus of bringing women into a more productive role in society. Of course, any change brings trouble and anxiety with it and the women's movement is no exception.

Older families, especially, may be strained and weakened by a sudden shift in women's roles. But the younger ones, the ones with fewer preconceptions, will take the change in stride.

The result, I am convinced, will be a stronger, more secure nuclear family.

My partner and I run a very successful furniture store together. But we'd make a lot more money if we could open some branches. Trouble is, that would mean going to a bank and taking out a loan, and my partner refuses to get into debt. How can I change his mind?

Assuming your facts are right, the way to start is to find someone else who's done what you've done and succeeded. Tell your partner the details of the story. And, if you can find several examples, so much the better.

If he still needs persuasion, you might arrange a meeting between you, your partner, and the businessmen who did what you're suggesting. Let your partner do the talking, if possible. Let him get out his doubts and fears.

If he's still reluctant, try it on the smallest possible scale. You might consider renting a place for a short period, with the option of extending if the business succeeds. Buy stock that can fit into the other store if the branch doesn't work out.

Incidentally, if you have trouble finding appropriate examples, an officer at the bank might be able to help.

From the process standpoint, what you have here is a traditionalist partner, one who's really comfortable in the self-limited environment he's made. If you're to wean him away, you're going to have to take small steps in order to constantly allay his doubts and increase his feeling of security by structuring information to help him through the resistance-testing phase.

I'm about to become a mother and I'm confused with all of the child-rearing theories I've heard. Can you tell me, from a LIFE-CONTROL *point of view, which is the best way to raise a child, permissively or strictly?*

Neither and both. It depends on the phase. Normally, children need some discipline during their introductory phase (until adolescence), just enough to make them feel secure and to prevent them from harming themselves; considerable discipline during resistance-testing (adolescence); and very little thereafter.

Parents should remember that they are the leaders of the family and that their responsibilities toward their children are very much the same as any leader's responsibilities toward the members of the group.

Mainly, parents should provide their children with a strong sense of security and stability, to allow them to undertake the changes that accompany and constitute growth and development.

Also, they should encourage their children to develop independently as they mature, since they won't truly be able to enter their own productive phase until they feel inner strength.

I'm the head of the English department at a large university. At the beginning of every semester, just when my work is heaviest, I'm besieged by the professors and instructors who work under me. They bring me all of their prob-

lems and make it hard for me to do my work. How can I get them off my back?

You won't be able to do that, at least not entirely. You may be able to set up a procedure in which your assistant handles most problems initially. But you'd better be available for important matters.

This is a classic resistance-testing period and group members are acting in the classic resistance-testing manner. As a leader, your responsibility is to be visible and available at all times. Nothing can better provide group members with the feeling that everything is under control.

If you lock the door or forcefully discourage interruption, you'll just be letting yourself in for more trouble later. You won't be solving any problems, especially your own.

I'm a single guy who just can't seem to sustain a relationship with a woman. Everything goes fine for a few months, then I get bored and look for someone new. Yet, I'd like to settle down and get married. Do you think I ever will?

You sound like you might be an introductory-phase personality, someone who craves excitement, who's always eager for something new. If that's the case, you may never settle down, even if you do get married.

My advice is to do some self-examination. If, indeed, you fit the above description, you have two choices: Either change, perhaps with professional counseling, or learn to enjoy yourself the way you are. Your choice depends on what you want out of life.

One boy in a class I teach is forever interrupting. He's not really a bad boy, or even a bad student. But he breaks up the flow of the class. What can I do about him?

It just may be that the boy doesn't have the proper skill levels. He may not understand what effect his interruptions have on the class and on his own education. He may be overeager for attention and recogniton. He may be hyperactive.

The way to deal with the boy is to program him, to teach him (privately, to avoid embarrassment) how to behave in the classroom situation. Then have him work on projects with two or three other children. The problem, very likely, is a lack of information and skills, not a desire to disrupt. Help him develop his skills and you'll probably soon be having him behaving more appropriately.

I'm divorced and remarried, happily. Yet, I keep thinking about my first husband. Why?

The family is the only group in which there is no such thing as temporary membership. Separation, divorce, even death doesn't exclude the member from the group, if only in memory.

Marriage partners, particularly, take much of their identity from each other. In a very real sense, they become each other—to a degree. They internalize each other. So, should they separate, they retain part of each other within themselves.

In a remarriage situation, the partners will also take part of their identities from each other and, eventually, the new partner's influence will predominate. But the old partner will never vanish from the mind completely.

I'm a supervisor at an ore-processing plant in the Southwest. I'm an easygoing sort who doesn't put much pressure on his men. Most of my crew likes me, I think. My opposite number is a hard-driving son-of-a-gun who's hated by all of his men. I know that for a fact. But his group outperforms mine. Should I change my style?

No. One of the prime characteristics of a good leader is his comfort with his own leadership style. If he doesn't feel secure with himself, he'll never be able to make the members of his group feel secure.

Your problem may be, however, that you're running your group so democratically that it doesn't feel it *has* a leader. Make sure your men know who the boss is. Make sure they know what you expect of them. My guess is that they'll do the best job they can. Maybe they already are.

I've been in therapy for six months and I think I've made some progress. But lately I've been feeling more and more depressed. It seems to me my therapy may be the cause. Maybe I should quit.

Probably not. My guess is that you've been in the introductory phase for most of the time you've been in therapy and that you're now in the midst of resistance-testing.

It's a very common pattern for patients to feel considerably worse during psychotherapy just before they break through into genuinely productive change. The reason is usually that they're confronting significant issues for the first time.

If you quit now, you're not likely to resolve your problems. If you continue, you may experience a substantial breakthrough in a relatively short time.

My husband and I have been fighting ever since we got married three years ago. My mother says all we need to solve our problems is a baby. Is she right?

Probably not. You're evidently in the resistance-testing part of your marriage. You're both still seeking to feel secure and stable within yourselves and within your relationship. You haven't yet made a final commitment to the marriage.

Having a child in this circumstance forces the parents to make that commitment, whether or not they're ready. It's analogous to the leader who refuses to allow his group to do any acting-up, saying, "Okay, that's enough of that. Let's get down to work."

So, in this situation, the infant symbolically assumes the leadership role. Man and wife are asking it to provide the security and stability they've been so far unable to offer each other. It's an unnatural, unnecessary, and impossible burden in most cases.

Usually, the result will not be a clean, sure move into the productive phase, but a grudging, reluctant shift that leaves the original resistance-testing issues still simmering, complicated by the content problems inherent with a new baby.

I'm the owner of a women's dress shop. We've just moved across town, into a big, new building. Until we moved, I thought my staff was terrific. And there was no question of their integrity. Now they're goofing off. Why? Can I do anything short of firing them? They're valuable employees —or they were.

My guess is that your staff is doing some resistance-testing. Remember, they've just undergone a change, moving from one building to another, across town.

That may not sound like much, but it could have meant an extensive change in habits for some of them—waking up at different times, taking different routes to and from work, switching restaurants for lunch, etc.

By loafing, your employees are resistance-testing, expressing their anxieties, asking for guidance and reassurance. They need to know someone is in control of events.

The danger here is the possibility of overreacting. It would be all too easy to express great disappointment in their behavior. If you did that, you could not only lose valuable employees, but also create a permanent atmosphere of distrust.

Instead, I'd first try telling everyone that you know the change caused problems for some, even though there were many good things to it, too. Make it clear that your door is always open if anyone has problems he wants to discuss. Then make it clear that you intend the new store to be run in a businesslike manner, just as the old store was. If necessary, tighten up on your supervision. The move probably deprived them of close contact with you.

Remember, as a leader, when something goes wrong in the group, it's your fault half the time.

I know I'm only eighteen and Bob is just nineteen, but we love each other and we want to get married. Why shouldn't we?

Almost always, both partners in a teen-age marriage are in the resistance-testing periods of their overall life cycles. And, when they get married, they quickly find themselves in the resistance-testing phase of that relationship. They face anxiety and change wherever they look.

Very rarely does either teen-age partner have the inner stability to tolerate the resistance-testing of the other. The marriage quickly becomes a battleground, with both partners stepping on the other in an attempt to prove their independence. There is no sense of control or security.

So there's a good process reason for waiting until one or both partners is more or less through the resistance-testing phase before getting married. That way, the odds are better that the partners will be able to find the inner security they need before commitment. If you do get married, recognize that the difficulties you will have can be anticipated.

I have a subordinate who's full of ideas, but never follows through. What should I do with him?

What you evidently have here is a person with an introductory phase personality. Instead of concentrating on his liabilities, not being able to follow through, consider him for his assets, his steady stream of ideas. Find some job within your organization that calls for his skill. You'll both benefit.

My child was a perfect angel for the first thirteen years of her life. Now she's a rebellious hellion. Why? And what can I do about it?

Very often, a parent with a teen-age child says, "He's going through a phase." And the parent is absolutely right. The phase the child is going through is known as the resistance-testing phase.

When children enter this period, their parents act the way any leader does when confronted with group members in resistance-testing. They attempt to avoid it by overreacting or trying to stay in the introductory phase (preventing their children from confronting the major issues of adolescence); or withdrawing by surrending the leadership role, frequently to the child himself, letting him do whatever he wants without providing guidance.

Any one of these mistakes will cause trouble. But the most common parental mistake is parental overreaction, characterized by frequent and fairly severe punishment and an atmosphere of constant, intense conflict.

If you're a parent in this situation, my advice is to try to establish a détente as quickly as you can. Expect acting-up and allow for it. Don't match it with overreaction. Don't assume your child is becoming a monster.

Remember that adolescence is a time of tremendous change for a youngster, physically, sexually, socially, and intellectually. He or she will never again experience such total change. And remember that change automatically causes anxiety and acting-up, a request for guidance, direction, and reassurance.

To provide that guidance, be firm on important matters, especially when they involve potential danger for the child—drugs, alcohol, the car, sexual relationships, for example.

But remember that you and your child are not members of the same generation. What in your childhood may have been a situation fraught with danger may for this generation be essentially harmless.

Then, avoid crossing swords with your kids on major issues. Instead, set up battlegrounds where, if you're the loser, your children won't have a license to get into serious trouble. Devise rules that involve hair length, dress, how late the youngster can stay out, etc.

Whatever rules you set up, that's where you'll be tested first. And if you've set them up for issues that aren't life or death, it won't really matter if you're forced for some reason to give in. Either way, no one is hurt.

My husband feels he wants some sexual variety, but he doesn't want to sneak around and have affairs, he says. He wants us to have an "open marriage." The idea interests me and scares me at the same time. Does this mean our marriage is in danger?

Maybe, maybe not. If your marriage is in resistance-testing, open marriage may perpetuate the state of noncommitment. It encourages those who have outside liaisons to fantasize about changing partners, and it provides the opportunity.

On the other hand, open marriages are very often honest agreements that can decrease suspicion to some degree, while providing novelty for one or both partners.

In my view, open marriage—if it's to work—requires a stable, secure relationship, a productive-phase relationship. By definition, this relationship does not exist during the resistance-testing phase of a marriage.

Personally, I've never come across a couple that has been able to tolerate this arrangement for any length of time. One partner has sooner or later become disenchanted with the idea, or depressed over the other partner's needs and an inability to fulfill them within the marriage.

But, then, maybe the successful open marriages just haven't shown up in my office, since they had no reason to seek professional help.

I've been working at my job for five years now and I've been advancing steadily, both in terms of salary and position. But I'm so bored with it lately I can hardly drag myself into work. It just doesn't excite me any more. Should I change jobs?

What you have here is the primary problem of the productive phase. You're past the positive excitement of the introductory phase and the negative excitement of resistance-testing. Your satisfactions are more subtle now. You feel you need something new, to make you feel involved and interested again.

Before you impulsively change jobs, look at the rest of your life to see if you can find the necessary excitement there. It seems to me you're doing too well at work to sacrifice your progress so quickly.

Instead, consider a vacation, or even a leave-of-absence of three or four months. Consider an exciting new hobby. Ask yourself if this may not be the time to have another child. Look for new projects on the job, activities as different as possible as those you're already engaged in.

Once you've exhausted these alternatives, then think about a new job if the problem persists. But don't rush. And remember that while you'll find the excitement of the introductory phase in any new position, you'll also have to deal with resistance-testing and then the boredom of the productive phase after awhile.

I've just discovered that my husband of twenty-three years, my partner in life whom I've loved and helped and suffered with when we had problems, the father of our three children, is playing around with a twenty-four-year-old woman. And he's fifty! I'm thinking of seeing the divorce lawyer. Is that the right course of action?

Probably not. Obviously, the two of you have been in the productive phase of your marriage for years. You've made deep emotional investments in the relationship, and there's been a strong degree of identification with each other. You're part of him and he's part of you. A divorce would be tantamount to amputation.

Instead of taking so drastic and harmful (to both of you) a step, first examine what's going on here, in process terms. At the age of fifty, your husband is at one of the most common reevaluation points of his life. He's at a milestone. Many people think that age is the end of the middle years.

I've no doubt that your husband is worried, both about the future and the present. He doesn't know how much longer he's going to live and be healthy. Also, he needs to be reassured that he is still a vital and vigorous man, attractive and interesting to the opposite sex. He's feeling older.

Then, too, the two of you have spent a long time in the productive phase. After a time in this phase, the excitement inevitably diminishes. Part of that may be your fault, part his. Neither of you may be fulfilling the other's emotional and physical needs any more.

My advice is to treat this as productive-phase acting-up, if you can. Look at the episode as a request for reassurance and guidance, and provide what's requested. Give your husband the emotional support he needs. On the other hand, make it clear to him what you require from him.

Most of all, don't overreact by running off to the divorce lawyer (unless this is the last straw in a highly unsatisfactory relationship). The wise husband or wife in this situation—and it can happen to either spouse—should recognize that a single affair is not the end of the world, but that a divorce might be just that.

The day we got back from our honeymoon, we started to argue, my wife and I, and we haven't stopped arguing since. We've been at it for four years now. I've tried everything I know, even suggested marriage counseling, but to no avail. Maybe a divorce is the best answer.

Indeed, it may be. You and your wife have never made it out of the resistance-testing phase and it's starting to look like you never will. You don't have those years of success and happiness behind you that the couple did in the previous example, and you probably haven't internalized each other anywhere near as much. For that reason, a divorce might liberate you both and allow you to find another partner, hopefully one with whom you can move through resistance-testing rather quickly and establish a productive relationship.

I have three boys—eight, eleven, and fourteen. They come from the same family but they couldn't be more different. Why is that?

Of course, there are many factors here, genetic as well as environmental. But an important reason for the differences between children in the same family is the phase of the marriage into which they're born and during which they're raised.

Older children are usually the ones born into the family

when it's in the resistance-testing phase. They're often more achievement-oriented and more productive than their younger siblings, according to many studies. But they're also usually more anxious, more obsessive, more isolated, and more withdrawn than their brothers and sisters.

This is because they often play the role of tension reliever. Their parents use them to discharge pent-up pressures by shouting and yelling at them. So they're subjected to more demands and more tensions.

Children born and raised during a family's productive phase are likely to have an enriched socialization experience beginning early in life. They're likely to be more verbal than their siblings born earlier and have superior social skills.

They may have a fairly serious emotional problem a few years later, however, when the older siblings move out. They may experience this as a serious loss, unless parents figure out ways to ease the separation.

Children born late in a family's productive phase may not have as much contact with children of their own age as those born earlier. Their contact with their parents may be intensified and they may be treated as and act like adults at an earlier age, further separating them from their peers, unless parents make sure there are plenty of children for them to play with.

Late babies, those born to a family nearing the end of the productive phase, may not have the opportunities for growth that were available to their older siblings. The tensions of resistance-testing and the enriched socialization of the productive phase will be lost to them.

These children may also feel isolated. There may be serious communication gaps between children and parents. And the child's parents, being older than the parents of other children that age, may have generational differences that will impede the child's growth.

The only solution to this problem is to be aware of the process here and to make the necessary corrections—providing the youngster with other kids his own age to play with, recognizing generational differences, striving for good communication, etc.

Obviously, I could go on forever with these questions and answers. But now it's time for you to take over.

You have learned a system that will give you more control over your own life and the capacity to become a more effective leader as you interact with others.

I hope this knowledge will help make your everyday life more satisfying and rewarding, and that it will show you how to be more productive throughout all your days. More, I cannot wish you.